SO-AIN-849

Liberating Faith
Practices:

Feminist Practical Theologies
in Context

Liberating Faith Practices:

Feminist Practical Theologies in Context

Denise M. ACKERMANN and
Riet BONS-STORM (eds.)

Regis College Library
15 ST. MARY STREET
TORONTO, ONTARIO, CANADA
M4Y 2R5

BT
83.55
-L523
1998

PEETERS

ISBN 90-429-0003-2
D. 1998/0602/20

© 1998 Uitgeverij Peeters, Bondgenotenlaan 153, B-3000 Leuven

*For the women of
the International Academy of
Practical Theology*

TABLE OF CONTENTS

I

Introduction

Denise ACKERMANN and Riet BONS-STORM

This book has its origins in the 1995 conference of the International Academy of Practical Theology in Bern where it became clear that there were members of this Academy who were unfamiliar with feminist perspectives and their contribution to the formation of practical theology. Several women members of the Academy decided to contribute to a book that would demonstrate a variety of feminist practical theological perspectives, each firmly anchored in its particular context. The title of this volume, *Liberating Faith Practices: Feminist Practical Theologies in Context* illustrates our intent. We view practical theology as the theological discipline which is essentially involved with living, communicating and practising the life of faith. As women we bring our theological reflections on our experiences to our discipline as legitimate exercises in the doing of practical theology. We hope that our voices will be both disruptive of dominant male discourse as well as liberating for those who have an interest in the reflections and actions of *all* people of faith.

Practical theology is probably the theological discipline least influenced by feminist voices. Why is this so? First, practical theology as a discipline is largely a fruit of modernity. When the hegemony of pre-modernity was waning, the question arose: who would undertake the task of the formation and guidance of the Christian church? The belief that individual congregations, as members of the larger body of the church, were progressing towards ever-improved, better functioning Christian communities, called for theologically equipped leaders, the clergy. The task of training these leaders fell to practical theology. As a discipline, it had to provide tools for the clergy which would enable them to lead, educate and counsel the local community towards the goal of the exemplary Christian body of believers.

The male was the subject of modernity. The male was also the subject of the clergy. The male clerical paradigm in practical theology not only barred women from the clergy but, as such, also excluded them from being theological subjects and actors.

Second, even when the clerical paradigm in practical theology was broadened to include the whole *ekklesia*, many churches still considered only male persons to be practical theological agents. Male clerics acted and spoke as pastors to their flock consisting of men as well as women. The pastor was purportedly trained in the art of listening to his sheep, male as well as female. Empathy became important. A pastor was supposed to enter into the feelings of others, and to emphasize the importance of emotions. As emotions were widely (mis)understood as being chiefly women's terrain (while men were considered the more rational beings), practical theologians, who were concerned with equipping pastors with tools for their trade, now had to enter into the 'feminine' field of emotions. Many practical theologians, far more than systematic theologians and biblical scholars, understood themselves as having developed their 'feminine self'. This 'empathic feminine self' proved to be yet a further barrier. These practical theologians, satisfied with their newly acquired skills, did not deem it necessary to listen to women colleagues or to acknowledge their particular skills and their insights into women's experiences and struggles to live lives of faith.

Third, practical theologians often display insecurity about their identity and purpose as theologians. Endless debates occur at conferences around issues of identity. These debates are not necessarily uninteresting and they do demonstrate a process of continuous self-reflection and theorizing not often found among other theological disciplines. Yet they also serve as distractions from the pressing concerns of practical theology in a world full of want and show an unwarranted concern with finding unanimity in a discipline which, by its very nature, is dynamic and transforming.

There is, unfortunately, a further negative effect of this continuous crisis of identity. When the white, well-educated men who traditionally sit around the practical theological table are insecure about their identity, they are not eager to let 'others' join them. The addition of the unfamiliar and the unexplored at the table, renders their identities more vulnerable and unsettled.

In this book, the voices of 'proximate others' are heard.[1] Women are both like and also different from the dominant group. The authors, all women, are all well-educated and are all white. There are no voices of black women in this book. Despite invitations to several black women practical theologians, we were unsuccessful in securing their participation in this project. This has sorely limited the variety of voices from different contexts in this book and has deprived us of hearing the perspectives of those who know 'otherness' in all its complexity. The 'whiteness' of this book raises a number of questions which call for ceaseless self-examination. One such question is that of tokenism. Women know what it is to be overloaded with academic responsibilities because they spend so much time being the token 'woman's voice' on endless committees and conferences, meetings and commissions. How much more so for black women in academic environments which are overwhelmingly white? Another question raised is that of strategies for self-empowerment. We understand the need for women who have experienced discrimination on multiple levels to make their own spaces, to seek their own ways and to draw up their own agendas. As white women we accept responsibility for this reality and we continue to hope for future collaboration across barriers in the cause of greater diversity in practical theological discourse.

As all the articles in this book are from feminist perspectives, they include either an explicit or implicit critique of reigning, dominant models of practical theology. The nature of practical theology is, as we have argued, largely determined by its history. In the interests of the future of our discipline as an inclusive, dynamic one

[1] This term was used by Herbert Anderson in his address entitled 'Seeing the other whole: A habitus for globalization' at the International Academy for Practical Theology's conference in Seoul, South Korea, on 22 April, 1997.

concerned with transformative practices, we summarize a feminist critique of reigning models in the following four points.

First, the lack of gender, race or class analysis in practical theological theorizing militates against the reflection/action mode of practical theology being employed in such a way that the lives of those who are absent from the male-dominated discourse are touched. This lack of analysis not only raises issues of efficacy but also issues concerning the roles of power and difference and their relation to the politics of the academy, the interpretations of situations and the making of meaning. Second, the hegemony of white males in the writing and teaching of practical theology silences the voices of women and other marginalized and oppressed people. In our countries, the Netherlands and South Africa, practical theology is overwhelmingly a male-dominated discipline. When one looks at the nature and composition of faculties, publications and societies concerned with practical theology, this point is proved. Not least of all, the International Academy of Practical Theology is itself prodigiously male. Practical theological theorizing must be relevant to the material concreteness of the lives of those who inhabit the ever-increasing outer circles of discourses.[2]

Third, practical theology, which sees itself as focusing primarily on the training of the (preponderantly male) clergy, does not accord sufficient significance to the communicative actions of the majority of people of faith. These include a growing number of articulate and critical women, who today find themselves either on the fringes, if not outside, the institutional church for a variety of reasons. Women's voices do not impact on this inner circle of practical theology, except as objectified themes of study, for example, on how to counsel the battered wife. Women's concerns and women's faith praxis remain obscured.[3]

---

[2] 'Outer circles' as a metaphor, refers to all who do not take part in the dominant discourse of the inner circle. The outer circles are free to expand and grow while at the same time encircling the constricting inner circle.

[3] To illustrate the point: the long fought battle for the ordination of women to full-time ministry, enjoyed scant support from male practical theologians; sermons and teaching by male clerics on the endemic sexual violence against women are as scarce as the proverbial fairies' teeth.

Finally, methods of empirical research employed by the operationally-centered models of practical theology, which purport to advance emancipatory knowledge, must take cognizance of feminist research methods in which the social construction of gender is placed at the centre of the enquiry.[4]

Feminist research methods view gender, in all its complexities of race and class difference, as vital to the shaping of consciousness, skills and institutions. Gender analysis becomes a basic organizing principle of feminist research. Self-reflexiveness is seen as an essential aspect of transformative research, requiring an awareness of one's own position. Emancipatory feminist research aims at being reciprocal, encouraging deeper self-reflection and understanding on the part of the researched and the researcher in a relationship of mutual subjectivity. The goal is to generate new theories from experience for new emancipatory praxis. Patti Lather writes: 'By resonating with people's lived concerns, fears and aspirations, emancipatory theory serves an energizing catalytic role. It does this by increasing specificity at the contextual level in order to see how larger issues are embedded in the particulars of everyday life. The result is that theory becomes an expression and elaboration of progressive popular feelings rather than abstract frameworks imposed by intellectuals on the messy complexity of lived experience'.[5]

While feminist critiques of male-centered models of theology are necessary to expose shortcomings and contradictions, they are not sufficient for the ultimate goal of the liberation of women and the transformation of our religious structures in their different contexts.

---

[4] For a discussion on what is distinctive about feminist social enquiry, see Sandra Harding, *Feminism and Methodology* (Bloomington, Indiana University Press, 1987). On the goals of feminist research, see Renate Duelli Klein, 'How to do what We want to do: Thoughts about Feminist Methodology', in G. Bowles and R. D. Klein (eds.), *Theories of Women's Studies* (London, Routledge, 1983), pp.88-104. See also Maria Mies, 'Towards a methodology for Feminist Research', in E. Altbach, et al. (eds.), *German Feminism: Readings in Politics and Literature*, (Albany, State University of New York Press, 1984) pp. 357-366 and Patti Lather, *Getting Smart: Feminist Research and Pedagogy with/in the Postmodern* (London, Routledge, 1991).

[5] Lather, *Getting Smart*, pp. 61-62.

The authors in this book are fully aware of the need to spell out new visions for transformed praxis and revised theories in practical theology. This they do. They speak out of their particular experiences in their different contexts, while holding on to hope for new and better ways of being and doing. These hopes are translated into proposals for transformative practices. No unity or conformity is aspired to in this book. The common ground is white women claiming a seat at the table of practical theological discussion.

Despite the variety of contexts and approaches in this volume, certain themes frequently appear which show a correspondence of intention within contexts of great diversity. The epistemological significance of women's experiences in doing practical theology is common to all contributors. The desire for just and liberating praxis within clearly stated contexts is a further central concern of the contributors. All contributors probe the potential of practical theological theorizing and, in so doing, enlarge not only the scope of our discipline, but also enrich the promise that theology can contribute to a better world.

In chapter two, Riet Bons-Storm sets out her particular understanding of practical theology as 'faith lived in context' against the background of practical theology in the Netherlands. Raising questions of truth and context, she examines what it means to live with difference-in-equality. Her ethical and theological 'measuring rod' for her understanding of practical theology is the most vulnerable member of human society, the child. With this hermeneutical point of departure in mind, she links the practice of practical theology to the dialogue of faith as a dialogue between equals.

In the next chapter, Pamela Couture uses the camera as metaphor for exploring her view of pastoral care in the context of the United States of America. The camera as the 'social ecology of care', is the means of interpreting social change and in particular looks at practices of care. Fitting the different lenses of feminist, Wesleyan and practical theology to her camera, she analyses the dysfunctional areas of her society. This exercise enables Couture to suggest changes to the practices of pastoral care in which her concern for child neglect and poverty is central.

In chapter four, Carol Lakey Hess explores practical theology as midwife to just community life. Drawing on Carol Christ's insights, she proposes a practical theology which embodies passion, empathy and judgement. Passion translated as communicative justice, empathy which is born in grassroots sharing among women, and judgment which is exercised in mutuality in prophetic communities, all contribute to just conversations which enlarge our perspectives, enabling us to live justly with difference.

The concern with justice is also picked up by Denise Ackermann in chapter five. Against the background of the Truth and Reconciliation Commission in South Africa, she sets out a feminist theology of praxis in which healing is a core concern. Dealing with issues of accountability and forgiveness, she suggests communal lament in small communities of faith as vital to the healing of her society.

The theme of lament crops up again in chapter six where Nancy Eiesland combines insights of sociology with Iris Marion Young's analysis of justice, to describe the barriers facing women with disabilities. Her theological reflections center on what it means for a woman with disabilities to be made in the image of God. She concludes by outlining the implications of a liberatory theology of disability for the community of faith.

In chapter seven, Elaine Graham examines the relationship between culture and gender in Britain today. Her point of departure is the belief that feminist practical theology emerges from the encounter of faith and practice in the form of values which are embodied and enacted to respond pastorally to women's changing circumstances. Graham explores the inclusive liturgical practices of the St Hilda Community as a pivotal contribution to innovative feminist praxis in the British context of pluralism.

In a somewhat different vein, Barbara Nicholas speaks as a theologian involved in the field of bio-ethics in New Zealand. In chapter eight, she examines the different stages in reproductive decision-making which women are faced with today as a result of modern technologies in genetic testing. The dilemmas and practical implications resulting from such choices are reflected on theologically, drawing on Gustavo Gutiérrez's writing on Job.

The last chapter in this volume is devoted to Bonnie Miller-McLemore's analysis of the evolving definitions of the study of religion and personality studies and their relationship with one another in the United States of America. By using three different readings, Miller-McLemore firmly anchors the study of religion in diverse moments of suffering, from which religious reflection emerges. The study of religion, she argues, needs to reject the pretence of objectivity; it is an exercise often without decorum and which calls for participation in radical truth-telling. Her article concludes by examining the problems and possibilities for the field of religion and personality studies, in the light of the preceding understandings.

In conclusion, most contributors have added select bibliographies of interest for all concerned with the task of exploring the many facetted nature of feminist practical theologies. We acknowledge with gratitude the many hours of work Ilse Ahrends and Ria Kuipers put into the final editing of this volume. The photograph for the cover was taken by Joost Bons and we also thank him for his willingness to help us in this project. Women's work is often invisible, but everywhere on the surface of this earth women are on their way to provide life-sustaining food and medicine to the people they feel themselves responsible for. In this way we, the authors of this volume, worked together to bring life-sustaining food to communities of faith, each in its particular context.

II

Putting the little ones into the dialogue: a feminist practical theology

Riet BONS-STORM

My context

I work as a professor of Women's Studies and Pastoral Theology in a university in the Netherlands. The Netherlands is a small, relatively rich, densely populated country. Due to its colonial past it has many citizens of colour: we are a multi-racial, multi-cultural and multi-religious society. The 'One Truth' of the predominantly christian Netherlands has been shattered. We live together as 'others' in great diversity.

After a few decades of socialist government, when social security was an important concern for all, we have for the last 15 years had a liberal/christian democratic government. Money spent on social security, health insurance, and on the growing number of unemployed, is increasingly considered money thrown away on 'coloured' strangers, on lazy people who do not want to work and probably buy drugs, or on unproductive weak, old people. A 'no-nonsense' politics of money-making silently proclaims the healthy, strong, hard-working businessman as the ideal of humanity. Women are surreptitiously led back into caring professions with low wages and low prestige, coaxed into the unpaid caring substructure of being a wife and mother, or into an 'emancipated' life in the competitive market place, which often leads to the double burden of being a professional woman and a caring wife and mother.

The obvious victims of these political ideologies are children. The christian-democratic party gallantly defends the nuclear family. It ignores the fact that most Dutch families (and for that matter, families all over the world) are not nuclear families in the traditional sense, that is a money-earning father in the outside world and an emotionally always available mother at home. Maintaining the traditional nuclear family mystique despite the changing ways in which many women view themselves, creates an avalanche of broken marriages and guilt feelings among women. Children growing up in the climate of these broken or stressed nuclear families cannot develop a strong enough sense of basic trust.

Such is the situation in the Netherlands, an affluent society. In poor countries the phenomenon of 'street children', homeless young boys and girls, desperately trying to stay alive doing odd jobs, stealing and prostituting themselves, cannot be ignored. Daily the images of wandering groups of refugees are seen on our television-screens, mostly composed of women, the elderly and of many children. How will these children grow up?

This phenomenon of neglected, disoriented children, coupled with growing anger at the increasing injustices shown towards all those who are not strong or able enough to make money, is missing in the practical-theological contextual analysis at Dutch universities. In my field of interest in practical theology, namely pastoral theology and practice, attention is mainly focused on the problems of individuals, understood as problems of individual theological and psychological adjustment to a 'normal' or 'God-willed'order.

I live and work as a feminist. I contend that the meanings given to sex and gender by the dominant discourses in society are important components in the making of personhood. To a great extent they determine people's views and standpoints. Although I have not been violently oppressed, I have a lifetime's experience of discrimination, of knowing that a woman has less authority to speak and to be heard than has a man. The voices of many women, together with their valuable contributions to the formation of thought and practice are ignored or silenced. I have come to understand this phenomenon not so much as the vice of brutal men, but as a structural problem of our societies and churches, because they are constituted by patriarchal ideologies. In my life and work I have to acknowledge the fact that the power to decide what is true and good rests with men, namely white, well-to-do, often university-educated men, while women are still understood as intrinsically less trustworthy, less rational and as such, are called to more or less overt obedience[1]. This power imbalance eventually leads to violence against women, much of which is sexual in nature. The aim of the feminist movement is to analyse this situation of inequality and oppression and to end the suffering. Power differences among women have to be taken into account as well. According to the dominant ideology of our society and churches, being white, middle-class, privileged and highly educated, grants power over people who are black, poor and untrained in the accepted rational discourse. This is true for men, but it is also true for women. Women need to be alert to this reality.

In the Netherlands the feminist approach to theology emerged from the grassroots. It was born out of the Woman and Faith Movement. This movement started in the seventies when women of different churches began to talk together about their frustrations concerning the theology and the practice of their churches[2]. Their common painful concern was: how can our particular experience as women of faith in this society be expressed in words and actions? How can our faith become really redeeming and liberating for us in our diverse contexts as women? Many women saw a yawning chasm between the promise of redemption and liberation on the one hand, and the actual situation of marginalization and exploitation of women inside and outside the churches, on the other. This feminist approach to theology arose in the everyday-

---

[1] See Riet Bons-Storm, *The Incredible Woman: Listening to Women's Silences in Pastoral Care and Counseling*, (Nashville, Abingdon Press, 1996).

[2] Cf Lieve Troch, 'The Feminist Movement in and on the Edge of the Churches in the Netherlands: from Consciousness-raising to Womenchurch' *Journal of Feminist Studies in Religion*, 5:2 (1989), 113-128; Foka Brouwer, *Een Bééld van een Beweging: Onderzoek naar de organisatie van de Vrouw-en-Geloofbeweging in Nederland*, (Leusden, Dienstencentrum, 1991); Riet Bons-Storm en Diana Vernooij, *Beweging in macht: Vrouwenkerk in Nederland?* (Kampen, Kok, 1991).

life of women in their different contexts. Many of these women were and are not officially trained theologians, yet they ask questions which come from their need for liberation, and they articulate theology in their own voices, longing for the abundant life promised by the Divine.

This context raises the question of normativity. Does a laywoman, untrained in theology as it is taught in universities, have authority to articulate her truth about the Divine and about salvation and liberation? Many a member of the Woman and Faith-movement has been looked at sternly by her minister when speaking about new insights into faith and theology. 'But you are not allowed to think like this,' is the common response[3].

I am a (critical) member of the Nederlandse Hervormde Kerk (Dutch Reformed Church) which was formed at the time of the Reformation. I have, however, only one foot in this church. My other foot is in the Woman and Faith-movement.

Practical theology in the Netherlands

In my country, practical theology focuses on the official churches and their congregations/parishes. The 'ecclesiological paradigm' is dominant, often in the form of a 'clerical paradigm'. This means that the main question in practical theology is: 'what does the minister or priest have to do in this or that situation?'

Male-dominated practical theology is very reluctant to take sex and gender into account. My colleagues speak about 'people'. This denies the fact that there are no 'people'. There are only women and men in their different situations, and in their different positions of power or powerlessness in society and the churches.

---

[3] Riet Bons-Storm, 'Maar zo mag je niet denken! Over ruimte en richting in een feministische benadering van theologie en geloven' ('But you are not allowed to think that way! About room and direction in a feminist approach to theology and faith') in Riet Bons-Storm, Corrie Dijksterhuis, Martha Kroes en Eva Ouwehand, *Ruimte en Richting: Vrouwen op zoek naar veel betekenend geloof* ('s-Gravenhage, Boekencentrum, 1990), p. 31-55.

'The communicative praxis of the Gospel' ('communicatief handelen' in Dutch) is an important concept in Dutch practical theology. This praxis is understood as the reflected acts of rational subjects, be it of the minister/priest (as mostly is the case) or of laypersons. What is not taken into account is that persons without the power to speak, according to the dominant ideology, cannot be deemed to be 'acting' subjects. An analysis is needed of what denies a person subjectivity and authority. The conditions for being able to 'act' have to be named and acted upon. Only when the powerless are not excluded can one talk about praxis ('handelen') as the focus of practical theological reflection.

As a protestant, I work mostly with protestant colleagues in the context of protestant churches. The traditional theology of the Reformation and Barthian theology dominates the theological discourse in my church. Less dominant is a group of more liberal theologians, who have their roots in 19th century Modernity. Both dominant theologies find their normativity in the texts of the bible, each has its own hermeneutic. My debate with these theologies centers on the issue of normativity. Basic to my theology is the interpretation of the christian faith through concepts, models and metaphors which are in a critical dialogue with the interpreted events of the Jewish people as told in the First Testament and with the perceptions of Jesus' life and death as told in the Second Testament, and which are, at the same time, sensitive to the belief-systems women and men, children and adults, use in their contexts to make sense of their experiences in everyday-life[4]. The revelation of the Divine was and is directed to persons in history, and as such, revelation itself is of an historical nature. The golden thread through Divine revelations was and is the Divine's passion for justice and abundant life – with a special eye and ear for 'the little ones' – as seen in Jesus, the presence of the Divine. The 'critical' in my dialogue with the concepts, images and words of the two Testaments is based precisely on this passion for justice and abun-

---

[4] Cf Truman A. Morrison, *Free in the Tearing Wind.* (Lansing, Mi, The Bear Creek Press, 1992), p. 61.

dant life. For me, 'normative'is what enhances justice and love –
especially for 'little ones' – and what strives to lessen injustice and
the infliction of pain.

My understanding of practical theology

The focus of my practical theology is 'faith lived in context'.
This 'faith lived in context' combines at least three ingredients.
First, christian tradition as imparted through different theologies
and in christian education, Sunday school and sermons has an
impact on our faith. For many women these theologies sound as
though they are being articulated in foreign languages. This causes
feelings of alienation and despair. Second, the context in which we
live influences faith deeply. Third, the touch of the Holy Spirit, the
Divine-in-action-and-communication, opens women's hearts to
the longing for liberation from oppressing forces in their particular
contexts which destroy their hope for abundant life. The touch of
the Holy Spirit has to be honoured. It gives every woman the right
to be listened to as a theological agent.[5]

I am grateful to the writings of Gert Otto, who understands
practical theology 'as a critical theory of a religiously transmitted
praxis in society'.[6] For Otto this 'praxis' is broader than the
actions of church leaders or ministers. Practical theology reflects
on the practices of all members of the community of faith, as individuals and as members of a community, who live their faith in
society. They have to take decisions about the way they choose to
give expression and form to faith in their particular situations.

Practical theology is the theological discipline that tries to construct theories which answer the question: how can people, in their

---

[5] Cf Stephanie Klein, *Theologie und empirische Biographieforschung*, (Stuttgart, Verlag W.Kohlhammer, 1994), chapter I.

[6] Gert Otto, 'Praktische Theologie als kritische Theorie religiös vermittelter
Praxis - Thesen zum Verständnis einer Formel' in *Ferdinand Klostermann und
Rolf Zerfasz (HGB.), Praktische Theologie Heute* (München, Kaiser/ Grünewald,
1974), pp. 195-205.

different contexts and conditions, live as faithful people and contribute to the renewal of life – personal, communal, worldwide –
according to the longing of the Divine? For me, being faithful
means to live and eventually die in critical orientation to a christian
tradition in such a way that the ambiguities and the brokenness of
life can be endured, and life can be experienced as meaningful in a
trusting relationship with the Divine. Living in this world with one's
eyes open spells dread and despair. The brokenness of life in all its
aspects cannot be ignored[7]. To be faithful one needs stories that go
against the grain because they do not gloss over the dread and
despair but give a vision of hope. To be faithful one needs to have
imagination, to imagine a different order, a new earth. In the Second
Testament I read that of faith, hope and love, love is the most
important. But nowadays I think that hope is the most needed
virtue. Hope nurtures the courage to love, that is, to be open to others and to see the best in them and to cherish them without being
afraid. Without hope in the midst of dread there cannot be faith.
Faith is fundamentally trust (the Greek 'pistis') in something or
somebody that encompasses our despair and dread in the wider context which we call 'the Divine' or God/dess. We come to that trust
by trusting others: those in the tradition, who tell us of their experiences of despair, hope and faith and those who live with us now in
our world. Hope, trust and faith give people courage to look at
themselves and the world critically, honoring the values as ascribed
to the Divine in the Christian tradition and living accordingly. As I
have written previously, for me, the Divine, whom I call God/dess,[8]

---

[7] I agree with the German practical theologian Henning Luther (*Religion und
Alltag: Bausteine zu einer praktischen Theologie des Alltags,* Stuttgart, Radius
Verlag, 1992, p. 27 ff), when he argues that the main function of religion is not
the search for meaning that harmonizes the brokenness of life or 'masters' contin-
gencies. Jewish and Christian religious traditions explicitly acknowledge the brokenness and give room to despair; for instance, in the Psalms, and in Jesus' cry at
the cross: 'My God, why have You forsaken me?'

[8] When speaking about the Divine, I use 'God/dess' as a linguistic device to
acknowledge the Divine as gender-inclusive: female and male. When I refer to the
Divine as expressed in traditional theologies, I use the word 'God'. Cf. my book
The Incredible Woman (see note 1), chapters 1 and 6.

stands for a passion for justice and abundant life for everybody: all who are oppressed and 'little' in the first place. According to tradition, the Divine Her/Himself touches us and gives us visions of hope and promised lands that only can be reached through deserts.

I want to stress the point that practical theology is about people in their various conditions: women, men, poor, rich, old, young, white, black, lesbian, homosexual, heterosexual, disabled, or not disabled and those who are more or less involved in a community of christian faith. Every person has a 'position' in society which, according to the dominant ideology, involves a certain amount of power and authority to make meanings that are perceived as plausible, or 'true'. These positions, with their power and authority, are ordered in a hierarchical manner, as imaged by a ladder. The more power-rendering factors a person has, the higher s/he sits on the ladder. Power-rendering factors in my society, church and university include being male/fatherly, having money, being white, being university-educated, being able-bodied and being heterosexual and having a traditional family. It is very clear that the current social-cultural climate marginalizes and silences people according to their lack of one or more of these power-rendering factors. Theology is deeply influenced by this social-cultural climate. The group who has the power to speak and be heard in practical theology hardly includes women, poor people, blacks, people who lack official education, homosexuals, the disabled, old and weak people and young persons.[9]

This fact is very important if one contends, as I do, that a community of faith[10] is the locus where the dialogue of faith takes

---

[9] The situation in the International Academy of Practical Theology makes this clear. Most members are white and have many power-rendering factors. There is a small minority of women, non-Western and black persons. Nevertheless, the 'speakers' and the people considered most electible as board-members, are white men.

[10] I prefer to speak about 'community of faith', which includes congregations and parishes, the members of a certain church or denomination, as well as the community of christians worldwide. This term also refers to communities of faith that transgress the boundaries of congregations, parishes, denominations and even christianity as a whole, such as interfaith-groups. A Woman and Faith-group can be understood as a community of faith, although it transgresses the boundaries of parish, congregation and denomination.

place among people who from their particular situations, look for visions of hope and orientation for their lives. A dialogue is not the same as a discussion or a debate. In a dialogue the difference of opinions is acknowledged and taken seriously. The aim of the participants is not to convince or defeat one another, but rather to understand one another. A dialogue is a qualified conversation, where people meet one another in a respectful manner to try and grasp what divides and what unites them and above all, to understand what inspires them. The basis of dialogue is the conviction, that the One and Only Truth cannot be known, because everybody is limited by her/his own context, position, viewpoint and interests. In dialogue these limitations can be reduced, viewpoints can be broadened and, eventually, interests shared. Perhaps one person's vision of hope can touch the other's vision of hope. Belief in the possibilities of the 'other' is the breeding ground of dialogue.[11] The dialogue of faith goes on in various ways, for instance in the preaching and discussing of a sermon and, explicitly, in pastoral care. The question of practical theology can be framed as follows: how can the dialogue of faith be continued in a meaningful, inspiring and fully participatory way which includes the voices of the powerless?

In my theology the notion of the priesthood of believers as the living stones of the house of faith acts as a leading concept. This concept was alive in the first christian communities, as testified to in I Peter 2. Behind this concept is the conviction that every person has knowledge of the Divine, because the God/dess longs to be known by all who look for Her/Him.[12] The possibility of direct, personal knowledge of the Divine does not mean that knowledge of the Divine is only possible for those who have special experi-

---

[11] Cf A.W.Musschenga, *De dialoog kritisch bezien,* (Baarn, Ten Have, 1983); P.Freire, *Pedagogy of the Oppressed,* (New York, Herder and Herder, 1971).

[12] Contrary to Stephanie Klein (*Theologie und empirische Biographiefor- schung* p. 45) I do not build my argument about the importance of the faith of laypersons on the assumption of an 'instinctus fidei', an instinct of faith. Klein's argument has an essentialist ring to it. To contend, as we both do, that the Divine will write Her/His law in human hearts (Cf. Jer. 31:33; Ez. 36:27), is an act of faith, not a reference to a factual situation.

ences that make them 'born again'. What I mean by 'knowledge of the Divine' is a conviction, developed in the particular situation and context of a person and influenced by a particular branch of christian tradition, that God/dess lets Her/Himself be known: implicitly, surreptiously; at times hidden and at times revealed.

The problem of normativity

What do I accept as the truth, as my ultimate point of orientation when I do practical theology? We need a concept of truth, that is based in women's own contexts, but that also gives us a basis for dialogue with others. A 'truth' can be understood as the ultimate value, which becomes the point of orientation of one's endeavours to give meaning to all one's experiences. Therefore truth is contextual. Taking over a truth from another context means to live in conflict and pain between one's own truth and the imposed truth of a dominant discourse. This painful conflict is confusing and very tiring. One needs allies and dialogue partners to really find out where one's own truth lies, and to analyse the relationship of this truth to the imposed truth of dominant discourse. Women's particular 'truth' comes into being when women analyse their marginalization. From their position at the margins they perceive those who are even less heard and more neglected and hurt than they are: children.

Nobody has privileged access to 'the way things really are', that is to ontological reality.[13] Truth can be understood as the road towards liberation from oppression and alienation, through changing landscapes and changing contexts. It is an avowed truth of where one stands 'for the time being'. This 'being' understood as being-in-reality has, however, to be understood fully. For me it means realising who one is, where one is, what the ultimate value is by which one lives and how conditions in this context lead to

---

[13] Cf Susan Thistlethwaite, *Sex, race, and God: Christian Feminism in Black and White*, (London, Geoffrey Chapman, 1990), pp. 12 ff.

despair as well as to possibilities of hope. One is never alone in a place. An awareness of where one is includes an awareness of relations with others and the relations of power that exist in that place. 'Truth for the time being' means awareness of the values at stake in a certain time and place, knowing where one's own ultimate commitment lies and practising these commitments. With Adrienne Rich I believe truth depends on the decision:

> With whom do you believe your lot cast?
> From where does your strength come?[14]

Truth has to do with one's survival with dignity, tested against the survival with dignity of the other. This particular, situated truth has to be brought into dialogue with other truths from other discourses, forming an ongoing dialogue about what could be a shared truth and thus a shared normativity. This dialogue is not an intellectual exercise, but a matter of survival in solidarity. It is a matter of making ethical decisions, a matter of learning to live with difference-in-equality.

My canon, my 'measuring rod', for the texts of truth and life, in or outside the tradition, is: can they be heard as liberating, challenging and inspiring for the most vulnerable, for the children? Do our thoughts and our practices bring them further along the way to a world of faith and hope where they can grow up without violence, hunger or refugee camps?

The child as a leading image[15]

In the Hebrew Bible the poor, the widows, the aliens and the orphans are used as metaphors for the oppressed and marginalized, who are central to God/dess' attention, love and passion for jus-

---

[14] Adrienne Rich, *Sources,* (California, The Heyeck Press, 1983), p. 12.
[15] Cf Herbert Anderson & Susan B.W.Johnson, *Regarding Children: A new respect for childhood and families,* (Louisville, Ky, Westminster John Knox Press, 1994) and Rita Nagashima Brock, 'And a little child will lead us: christology and child abuse' in Joanne Carlson Brown and Carole Bohn (eds.), *Christianity, Patriarchy, and Abuse,* (New York, The Pilgrim Press, 1990).

tice.[16] These metaphors have lost some of their ability to shock us into action. We need new metaphors which disclose new dimensions of human power and energy. For this reason, I see 'the child' not only as the real child, growing up in this world, but also as a metaphor. A child is small, vulnerable and dependent on others. Yet a child has wisdom and it looks at the world with eyes, which are not yet clouded by ideologies. A child can have fun without being hampered by selfconsciousness and embarrassment. A child embodies new life, the promise of the future. Like adults, a child needs others. Communities of faith of old testified that when the day comes that the earth shall be filled with the knowledge of the Divine, even a baby and a 'weaned child' shall play near a nest of poisonous snakes and not be hurt (Isaiah 11). In the three synoptic Gospels, (Matthew 19, Mark 10 and Luke 18), the story of Jesus blessing little children is told. The message is: 'Whoever will not receive the Kingdom of God like a child will never enter it'. Jesus puts his arms around a child, places the child in the middle of his disciples, and says: 'Whoever welcomes this child in my name, welcomes me' (Matthew 18, Mark 9 and Luke 9). This Jesus does in answer to the disciples' question: 'Who is the greatest in the Kingdom of Heaven?' 'The least is the greatest,' says Jesus. The least is a child. Jesus identifies with this child's vulnerability, smallness and naive wisdom. I am reminded of the story of Jesus' birth. The full theological meaning of the Christmas-story cannot be grasped if the babyhood of Jesus is merely viewed as the rather endearing foreplay to a life which culminates in death on a cross. The adult Jesus is usually understood as the true image of humanity. An adult male, roughly 33 years old and in the prime of life, becomes the true image of humanity. According to Luke, however, the first christian communities of faith witnessing to their belief in Jesus of Nazareth as the Messiah, represent this Messiah as a vulnerable baby bringing new life and hope in times full of

---

[16] It is important to note that the widow, and not the widower is mentioned in biblical texts. This bears witness to the fact that in ancient communities of faith, women, more than men, became victims of the reigning ideology and organization of societies.

oppression and suffering. The Messiah is also a vulnerable child dependent on and needing others.

When I was young I had no doubt that the child who was the focus of Jesus' attention was a girl. Subsequently in Sunday school and in sermons I learned that it was a boy. If Jesus were to be in my country today he would make a little girl the center of attention (and perhaps in fact he did this in Galilee). She, more than a little boy, is the metaphor of marginalization and vulnerability in our societies.

With the child as point of departure, I want to explore a practical theology that takes the child as a leading image. The child represents all those who do not have a voice of their own and who are marginalized and excluded from the dialogue of faith. If we were to enter the dialogue of faith as 'children', knowing that we are vulnerable and needy yet eager to 'grow up', willing to allow ourselves to be lead by our imagination, hoping that we can trust others, eager to learn and eager to play, theology would change.

The practice of this practical theology

How can the dialogue of faith as a dialogue between equals, vulnerable and open like children, become the practice of communities of faith? Reflection on this question has its impact on the whole life of the community of faith, on its liturgy, preaching, pastoral care, christian education and the sharing of material goods (diakonia). Rebecca Chopp argues that 'practice' can be understood as 'a pattern of meaning and action, that is both culturally constructed and individually instantiated'. Practices involve embodied actors.[17] The dialogue of faith in practice is more than just a discussion about faith. Its motivation and its goal are given theological meaning, as I have endeavoured to do in the previous sections of this article. The shape the dialogue of faith takes depends on the situa-

---

[17] Rebecca Chopp, *Saving Work: Feminist Practices of Theological Education*, (Louisville, Ky, Westminster John Knox Press, 1995), pp. 15-16.

tions and positions of persons in a particular culture. In contexts where groups of people – for instance women – are not heard by the dominant groups, these people will need first to dialogue about faith among themselves, to strengthen their voices. The language, the circumstances and the topics may vary. The motivation and goal remain the same: to strengthen the community of faith in its calling within its context, and to renew this context according to the longing of God/dess, until justice becomes abundantly present.

Together with Henning Luther I argue that all christians, whether they are heavily engaged in a community of faith or barely able to call themselves 'christian', have an incipient theology of their own.[18] In most churches laypersons are seldom invited to express their theologies in their own words. I am convinced by my experiences and by my belief in the ongoing revelation of the Divine, that even very shy and marginalized people can put their personal knowledge of the Divine into words and contribute to the dialogue of faith from their contexts, provided they feel that others are interested in dialogue and not merely critical.

In Woman and Faith-groups, for instance, women talk freely about their faith, their doubts, their ideas about the Divine. The situation is safe: no men are present, neither are there 'real' theologians, ministers or priests. Black women in the Woman and Faith-movement often opt for an all-Black group. The power-rendering factor of 'being White' gives white women hidden privileges[19] and an unconscious conviction of a greater authority than that of black women. Black women feel safer and speak their minds more freely in an all-black group. This is very difficult for white members of the Woman and Faith-movement who still have to learn how to handle their hidden privileges. Persons with only a few power-rendering factors and thus shy to speak about their personal knowledge of the Divine, can learn to share in the

---

[18] Luther, *Religion und Alltag*, p. 13.

[19] Cf Peggy Mackintosh, 'On the Invisibility of Privilege', *Peacework: A New England Peace and Social Justice Newsletter*, 205 (February 1991), 10-11.

dialogue of faith. Next to the traditional fields of practical theology (pastoral theology, christian education, liturgy, homiletics, etc.) increasing people's ability to share in the dialogue should be an important topic.

My experience of working together with women who are afraid to speak their minds in their communities of faith has taught me that, first of all, these women quite literally have to become used to raising their voices. They have to hear the sound of their own voice in groups or in conversation with another person to whom they give authority, like a pastor, a minister or a theologian. We practice speaking out, the act of 'raising one's voice', in a safe context. The second step is more difficult. A woman has to become convinced that she has something to contribute. To arrive at this point, she has to work through the effects on her sense of self of the traditional roles assigned to her in her socialization in a patriarchal society and church. As long as her role remains that of 'obedient daughter of a father, Fathers, or God the Father', she cannot speak her mind without being tortured by feelings of guilt and insecurity. Am I insufficiently educated? Am I stupid? Do I express myself badly? Am I too domineering, unattractive, emotional? These insecurities have to be taken seriously and not laughed off with cheap words of encouragement. She needs new stories, that give her the authority to speak. Practical theology should uncover these new stories. A woman needs an image of the Divine which will encourage her to raise her voice.[20]

In the same way children can be educated in faith not only as 'future consumers' of this faith, but also of persons who have the right to ask questions from their contexts and as persons who contribute to the understanding of the Gospel.

When muted persons in the community of faith are trained to contribute to the dialogue of faith, the role of the clergy will change. They become like midwives who remove obstacles which prevent faithful people from expressing their faith and they foster

---

[20] I elaborate on this topic in my book *The Incredible Woman*.

dialogue that is formative for a community of faith. Pastoral communication becomes a two-way traffic. Although a pastor is trained in academic theology and perhaps even in psychology, s/he is not necessarily more skilled in being faithful than a layperson is. To live life fully is a difficult task, both for an ordained person as well as for a layperson. Both have to learn to face the relevant questions and to look for answers to live by, while critically learning from questions and answers of individuals and communities of faith in their traditions. Pastoral communication should be a true dialogue of faith.

Preaching can enhance the dialogue of faith in a congregation. In the congregation where I live and worship lay-persons preach about once a month. Their sermons are prepared in small groups. If necessary, the lay-preacher asks the minister for advice on hermeneutical or exegetical matters. These sermons, mostly composed and delivered by people with little or no power to speak according to the dominant ideology, are as good as most of the sermons preached by ordained ministers. When an ordained minister preaches, s/he should prepare the sermon together with a group of parishioners. This will ensure that the sermon is communicable and relevant to at least part of the congregation, while at the same time training lay-people in the art of exegesis and sermon-making.[21] This can only happen if the dominant theology understands faith, not as a static object to be handed down unscathed by history and social conditions through the generations, but as a process that is the outcome of the willingness to relate experiences in everyday life to stories of the christian tradition, convinced that the Divine uses ordinary people to fulfil Her/His longing for justice and abundant life for all, and in particular for the Child in our midst.

---

[21] Cf Riet Bons-Storm, 'De theologische betekenis van de hoorders ofwel: de moed om een ogenschijnlijke chaos uit te houden' in *M. Bons-Storm en L.A. Hoedemaker (red.), Omwegen door de Woestijn* (Kampen, Kok, 1993), pp. 87-102.

ADDITIONAL BIBLIOGRAPHY

Campbell, Alastair V. *Rediscovering Pastoral Care*, London, Darton, Longman and Todd Ltd., 1986
Chopp, Rebecca S. *The Power to Speak: Feminism, Language, God*, New York, Crossroads, 1991
Chopp, Rebecca S. '*When the Center Cannot Contain the Margins*' in Don S. Browning, David Polk and Ian S. Evison (eds.), *The Education of the Practical Theologian*, Atlanta, Scholars Press, 1989, pp. 63-76
Couture, Pamela D. *Blessed Are The Poor? Women's Poverty, Family Policy, and Practical Theology*, Nashville, Abingdon Press, 1991
Elwes, Teresa (ed.), *Women's Voices: Essays in Contemporary Feminist Theology*, London, Marshall Pickering, 1992
Flax, Jane. *Disputed Subjects: Essays on psychoanalysis, politics and philosophy*, New York & London, Routledge, 1993
Glaz, Maxine and Moessner, Jeanne Stevenson (eds.). *Women in Travail and Transition: A New Pastoral Care*, Minneapolis, Fortress Press, 1991
Graham, Elaine and Halsey, Margaret (eds.). *Life Cycles: Women and Pastoral Care*, London, SPCK, 1993
Russell, Letty M. (ed.). *Feminist Interpretation of the Bible*, Oxford, Basil Blackwell, 1985

III

Feminist, Wesleyan, practical theology and the practice of pastoral care

Pamela D. COUTURE

I am a feminist, Wesleyan, practical theologian who asks, 'How can the practice of pastoral care be reconstructed to respond to emerging social challenges?' By 'pastoral care' I mean the divinely-given mutuality of care shared across laity and clergy on the basis of theological beliefs and values. Underlying the phrase 'emerging social challenges' are the questions: 'How is society changing? Who are we and who we are becoming in the midst of that change, and what might our relationship with God be and become in the course of that change?'

To focus these questions, I practice pastoral care. I am simultaneously a student of and a practitioner of pastoral care, even as I teach and write about pastoral care. As a teacher of a practice, I cannot be a practical theologian in mind only; I must also engage in some kind of embodied action. Practical theology reaches into our souls to engage our intellect and our bodies, our being and our doing. Pastoral care, as one practice of practical theology, draws on the methods and insights of science, but, in the end, is a creative act of imagination. It is an artistic practice which simultaneously engages human gifts, meets human need, and witnesses to a vision of life in which care for persons, for creation, and for God is central.

The art of pastoral care is somewhat like photography. Paradoxically, arts such as photography result from multiple forms of relationality and from careful, individual contemplation. In its relationality, photography becomes an experience between photographer and viewer, in which the photographer may offer to the viewer her expression of the world, allowing the viewer to see something the viewer had not seen before. But the viewer's experience of the photograph is independent of the photographer; the viewer's experience may be similar to that of the photographer's, or the viewer, looking at the same similar scene, may experience the scene very differently from the photographer or even see details the photographer had missed. Furthermore, the community of photographers is wide ranging: there are serious artists, technicians, and recorders of personal life. The sharing of work and commenting upon it creates community among artists and with a larger community. And yet, the care taken in the individual, artistic meditations of individual photographers significantly expresses an individual sense of self and contributes significantly to the communication among photographers and viewers.

As I practice care, I am aided by a structure, the social ecology of care, which becomes a camera through which I view social and individual change. The camera creates a frame so that I can focus more clearly on a part of the whole, seeing details I would otherwise miss. The adjectives feminist, Wesleyan, and practical are like lenses I attach to the camera through which I observe individuals, families and society. These lenses create overlapping yet distinct angles of vision. Like a camera and its lenses, social ecology, and feminist, Wesleyan, practical theologies are always means to an end other than themselves. The means, however are not neutral: the camera and its lenses form the limits and potentialities of a particular photograph, creating, in the process, particular values which will be highlighted in the photo. In creating a picture a photographer asks questions about the values that will be expressed when a scene or subject is framed in a unique way. By choosing the lenses of feminist, Wesleyan, and practical, I choose particular values as I use the camera of pastoral care to bring social change into view. Similarly, through the feminist, Wesleyan, and practical lenses of pastoral care I ask questions that express particular values: those values that promote love and justice in God's realm. The moments of social change that are slowed down and caught in the 'photographs' of care – the events in which actual care is shared – serve specific theological and ethical purposes: to describe the religious and moral questions with which individuals and cultures struggle; to make judgments regarding the human community's own idolatry and injustice; to express a faith which creates a pastoral, prophetic vision; and to create a means toward renewal and grace, healing and hope.[1] Therefore, feminist, Wesleyan, practical theologies connect structure and vision to guide the practice of the art of pastoral care.

To clarify: what is the camera – the social ecology of care – and what can it do? How do the lenses of feminist theology, Wesleyan theology, and practical theology activate the camera's potential? What norms – defined as values created from the camera's limits and potentials – are invariably embedded in the pictures of care that result? And what aim is served by the vision toward which those photographs aim?

The camera: the social ecology of care

The social ecology of care is a basic structure for interpreting social change with particular reference to the practices of care. In order to understand social change, sociologists have long studied the interactions of individuals, society, and culture. This framework has provided a starting point for practical theologians who study a wide range of social and ecclesiological practices. From the standpoint of the theologically-based practice of care we want specifically to ask how individuals and families are being hurt, helped, or shaped by social change. We want to know how individuals and families are showing strengths and resiliencies, revealing fragilities and even pathologies, and recreating norms. In order to do this, some pastoral theologians have explicitly added families to the framework of individuals, society, and culture.[2]

---

[1] Wilson Yates, *The Arts in Theological Education* (Atlanta, Scholars Press, 1987), pp. 25-26. In a study of the way in which art is integrated into the curriculum of the theology school, faculty with theological and ethical interests identified these four purposes as central to their interest in art. They summarized art as a basis for practical theology exceedingly well.

[2] See Larry Graham, *Care of Persons, Care of Worlds: A Psychosystems Approach to Pastoral Care and Counseling* (Nashville, Abingdon Press, 1992), p. 56.

Theologians reflecting upon the practice of pastoral care also have shown concern for the natural environment and the challenges we face within it. God's natural creation is a trust given to humanity which provides abundantly for humanity's needs. Creation is, in effect, God's way of caring for us. As a global society, how are we wasting or conserving that gift? As individuals and communities, how might that gift explicitly contribute to our abilities to care for one another? Nature, therefore, is also explicitly thematized in the social ecology of care.[3]

In the last few years, two other structures have emerged as highly significant for present social change as it hurts, helps, and shapes individuals and families. These structures include the rapidly shrinking welfare state and increasingly powerful global economic systems. In the United States as government services are reduced, politicians increasingly look to the church to care for the people that government says it cannot afford. In some cases, politicians who look to the church are simply trying to deflect responsibility for the welfare of individuals and communities from the political process to an unassuming party. In other cases, politicians are genuinely interested in promoting creative forms of church-state collaboration both in forming public policy and in creating new practices of care. Therefore, in the coming era, the re-creation of relationships between churches, local congregations, and federal and state governments will substantially shape new possibilities and limits for care.

This trend in the delivery of social services is fueled by the values and assumptions which undergird free market economics. Rational choice economic theorists believe that human beings will always make choices in their own best interests. They assume that individual self-interest will promote the common good and, therefore, they promote the value of individual self-sufficiency. Their philosophy advocates reducing public social services of all kinds in favor of privatization of care. The values of rational choice the-

---

[3] Graham, *Care of Persons*, p. 61.

ory now pervade non-economic disciplines such as psychology and even theology.[4]

These trends in the United States are particularly significant for women, for other industrialized nations, and for the developing Two-Thirds World. As public care declines, poverty rises, particularly for those with special conditions of vulnerability: children, the aged, the sick, the disabled. Since women provide the majority of unpaid, hands-on care for these groups of people, the loss of government service is likely to mean that the work of domestic care is transferred back to women. In addition, women in industrialized countries are employed in great numbers in welfare state social services; as social services are reduced, replacement jobs for women must be recreated through the private sector. In industrialized nations functioning community institutions can aid this transition; in communities where institutions are weak, poverty arises. Similarly, in most developing countries a stable infrastructure of national and community organizations has not been adequately built. Therefore, the resources for caring practices are very different than in western countries. Yet, as global economic philosophy influences developing nations, it will also shape the possibilities and limits for constructing pastoral care practice.

The decline of and change within government-sponsored care and the expansion of the premises of free market economics are rapidly becoming significant factors that create limits and possibilities for theologically-based care. Therefore, I propose that relationship between church and state and the influence of global economic philosophies be explicitly thematized in a social ecology of care.

A social ecological structure as the camera of care would then consist of the following parts:

---

[4] Pamela Couture and Richard Hester, 'Pastoral Care and God of the Market' in Pamela Couture and Rodney Hunter (eds.), *Pastoral Care and Social Conflict* (Nashville, Abingdon, 1992); see also Don Browning, Bonnie Miller-McLemore, Pamela Couture, K. Brynolf Lyon, and Robert Franklin, *From Culture Wars to Common Ground: Religion and the American Family Debate* (Louisville, Westminster/John Knox Press, 1997).

1) Individuals shaped by their genetic, biological, embodied selves; their personalities and individual development; their social traits, including ethnicity, race, gender, class, nationality and region.
2) Families and fictive kin: created through biological, affective, economic, and/or legal relationships, and organized into roles, responsibilities, and expectable systems.
3) Society: consisting of a variety of community institutions, including organizations such as schools, churches, service clubs, financial institutions.
4) Government-church relations: including its policy and social service sectors.
5) Culture: formed by assumptions, beliefs and values handed down through generations and remolded by the conditions in which each generation lives.
6) Economics: as it structures international relations and promotes a theory of the human being, especially as it defines the meanings of self-sufficiency, dependency, and interdependency.
7) Nature: which provides nourishment for and some threat to body, mind and spirit.

In order to think about the development of pastoral care in a changing context, here are the kinds of questions I would ask in each of the categories above (as an example I focus on the situation in Korea):

7) Nature: What distinctive resources does the natural environment offer to provide for abundance in human life? Are particular aspects of nature especially significant to the people? What in nature renews people? What in nature makes their life traumatic or difficult? How is nature being treated under the influence of economic modernization? Is nature being misused or polluted so as to corrupt the renewal the people receive from nature? How has nature traditionally spoken of God to the people, and what does nature today say about the presence of God?

6) Economics: How have economics changed? How does that change produce new limits or possibilities for institutions in a particular geographic context? Has the sense of self of the people in relation to the rest of the world changed as a result? Has economic change divided groups of people from each other, or brought them together? How is traditional culture reinforced and undermined by that change, and what are the advantages or disadvantages of this reinforcing or undermining?

5) Culture: What are the historically-formative events in Korea history? Who are the formative men and women? What values have they handed down to Korean men and women? How does the political division between the North and South create Korean consciousness? Who are the very privileged in Korea, what are their privileges, and how are those privileges kept in place? Who are the most vulnerable persons in Korea, why are they so vulnerable, and what forces keep them in place? What are the reigning assumptions about children in Korea? In the United States we hear great concern about the way that military presence or tourist trade in Asia has created a sex industry among women, including young girls. Are these women and their children the most vulnerable in Korean society, and should other populations receive public attention and support? What is required to care for these children and their families?

4) Government-church relations: In the United States the government of the church and state is 'separate' which means that the government is not allowed to fund the promotion of any one religion. Is does not mean that religious groups cannot speak to the practices of government – and they do. Some religious groups are more fully organized and get more publicity than others, but almost all religious organizations have some method for trying to influence government policy. The religious groups often do not agree about the way they want to influence policy, so many religious voices enter the religious discussion.

At present, however, a new opportunity is opening for churches. As government care through the welfare state decreases, churches are being sought by government agencies, such as the department of public health, to work with government agencies to provide services such as health education, immunizations, medical care clinics, etc. Government is likely to fund such church-based services in the future, as long as churches do not use these services in a formal way to solicit members. The developing situation has significant opportunities and dangers. Some groups, such as the United Methodist Bishops in their Initiative on Children and Poverty, are trying to hold government, public policy makers, and service groups accountable for the way they care for children and the poor and are trying to help the local churches develop new ministries to help children and the poor.

I know little about the relationship between church and government in Korea. Do church leaders present a moral vision of service and care for the vulnerable to their congregants and to people of privilege and power? When this is done, how is it done?

3) Community institutions: In the United States communities become poor when their institutions, such as churches, schools, and volunteer organizations fail. When these groups decline, intergenerational mentorship is increasingly absent. Through intergenerational mentorship older persons teach younger persons the skills for adult living, such as how to prepare for and find a job, where the jobs are, how to become a leader in the community, how to take on adult life tasks in financial and other domestic areas, and how to provide reciprocal care among generations. One of the most significant caring activities for the church is to reestablish community groups in which the generations can find mutual support.

In Korea what is the role of community institutions, particularly the church, in providing informal, intergenerational mentoring? Recognizing that many of these functions occur in the Korean extended family, how significant are teachers, ministers, Sunday School teachers, doctors, lawyers, and volunteers to the community?

2) Families and fictive kin: Family systems theory can help us understand the way families relate to one another over generations. A genogram charts who creates an alliance with whom, who

stops talking with others, how families work out their traumas by repeating the actions of forebears, and other patterns that are established in families. People who function as family but are not related legally should be included in this family map. This family mapping can also reveal the family's assumptions about gender, ethnicity, economics, and so on. What specific qualities do Korean families have in common, and what particularities does a particular family have?

1) Individuals: What are the particular struggles of this individual, sitting here before us, who must work out a life path, with the limits and possibilities created by all of the above?

The lenses of care: feminist, Wesleyan, practical

The social ecology of care is an abstract structure which I modified as I allowed the lenses to do their work on my own process of reflection. In other words, as I asked questions as a feminist, a Wesleyan, and a practical theologian, I needed to reinvent the original camera in order to see what these three lenses could most fully reveal.

The feminist lens

As a feminist, I questioned, 'What difference does gender make in our theology and our practices of care?' Although feminism is so diverse that calling myself a feminist could have many different meanings, this particular form of the feminist question shaped the social ecology of care in a particular way. I, like many psychologically-oriented feminists of the early eighties, had primarily concerned myself with gender as it determined sex roles. Carol Robb's essay in *Women's Consciousness, Women's Conscience* compelled me to broaden the structure with which I was then thinking about gender. In her assessment of different types of feminisms, Robb credited sex role feminism with calling attention to the 'essentially irrational basis for the sexual division of labor and

for gender-defined behavioral expectations ...'[5] Robb argued that
sex role feminism needed to articulate the way in which political
assumptions shaped sex roles and vice versa. So far, sex role feminism had not risen to this challenge. Even sophisticated versions
of sex role feminism, as in the work of Nancy Chodorow and
Carol Gilligan, failed to account for the way that sex roles differed
among races and classes of women and men. Because they
assumed that it would be possible to restructure sex roles within
existing social-political arrangements, these feminists of the early
eighties had not asked 'about the broad social-political conditions,
costs, and consequences of restructuring child-rearing practices to
allow for the recommended role redefinitions'.[6] As a result, the
social-political changes needed to support changes in family roles
were not adequately anticipated, and the needs of lower class
women were largely ignored.

Simultaneously, I saw the significance of Robb's point in the
lives of women counselees in my practice of pastoral counseling. I
have written about one of these women, Ellen, elsewhere.[7] As I
worked with Ellen, I realized that I needed to modify our interactions because basic economic and relational supports that I took
for granted among middle-class counselees were not in place in
her life. Ellen's situation called for a caring witness through a
practice more like social work than psychology. A practical feminist political perspective, such as that provided by social work,
was needed in theory and practice. A feminist political perspective
would not be meaningful for Ellen's or my life if it remained
abstract, in the genre of many feminist political writings. Rather, a
feminist political perspective could contribute to the mutuality of
care between Ellen and myself only if this perspective allowed her

---

[5] Carol S. Robb, 'A Framework for Feminist Ethics', in Barbara Hilkert
Andolsen, Christine E. Gudorf, and Mary D. Pellauer, *Women's Consciousness,
Women's Conscience: A Reader in Feminist Ethics* (Minneapolis, Winston Press,
1985), p. 226.

[6] Robb, 'Framework for Feminist Ethics'.

[7] Pamela Couture, 'Recreating the Web: Pastoral Care in an Individualistic
Society' in Jeanne Stevenson Moessner (ed.), *Through the Eyes of Women:
Insights for Pastoral Care* (Minnesota, Fortress Press, 1996).

experiential suffering to enter my academic scrutiny of the public policies which shaped the limits and possibilities for the care and lives of us both.

Once we discover the politics of care as it shapes the possibilities and limits for the lives of people in our own proximity, we must also ask questions about the politics of care in the lives of women and men beyond our immediate view. In our own region, how does the politics of care create the lives of people of different genders, races, ethnicities, classes, or stages in the life cycle? How does the politics of care connect us with or distance us from persons in other regions or nations? Once we admit that a significant politics of care exists, we must ask how we are called into a mutuality of care with persons within and beyond our immediate sight. Progress on these sorts of questions becomes an ethical necessity for feminist pastoral care.[8]

The Wesleyan lens

As a Wesleyan, I asked, how do we understand care as grounded in Wesleyan theology? I ask this question because I have found the general outline of faith as the Wesleys preached it and many Wesleyans after them developed it to make sense of the way I have experienced God acting in the world. I find the methods and concepts of Wesleyan theology, especially the Wesleyan understanding of the nature of God, to be ethically compelling. I do not ask this question because I assume that Wesleyan theology provides a more significant theological foundation for caring practice than do other theological traditions. Rather, every person will carry the uncritical assumptions of her faith (theological or not) into her caring practice. In the practice of care, I am more capable of genuine care when my faith assumptions are known to me so

---

[8] The term 'the politics of care' is applicable across caring disciplines. At Emory University, three major conferences have been held on the subject, the Politics of Care, planned by women from the schools and centers of women's studies, nursing, medicine, theology, public health, ethics, and an Emory-related hospital.

that I can critically reflect upon them. Every theological tradition can contribute toward understanding the theological roots of care. Sometimes, knowing a caregiver's theological tradition helps us understand why he or she constructs the discipline of pastoral care as he or she does, thereby promoting some caring practices rather than others.

As a Wesleyan, my theology of pastoral care is based on Wesleyan notions of God's grace. In fact, the practice of pastoral care *is* a means of grace for all involved. The formal means of sharing God's grace include, in traditional language, 'works of piety': devotional activities such as sharing the sacraments, studying the Scriptures, and praying privately and with others, and 'works of mercy', such as visiting the poor, the imprisoned, and the sick and advocating on their behalf. In contemporary terms, provisional means of grace would include engaging in practices which create an attitude of compassion, hospitality, and generosity in ourselves and which lead us to act on such attitudes. To engage in such practices on a regular basis is to practice pastoral care as a spiritual discipline.[9]

Particularly in the area of pastoral care where God's presence may or may not be explicitly acknowledged, we are aided by prevenient grace. The emphasis on prevenient grace is distinctive among Wesleyans. Through prevenient grace God reaches toward us, invites us into relationship, and struggles with us, before we are ever aware of it. If one truly believes in prevenient grace, everything changes. We are called to look to the entire created world for the formal and provisional means of God's grace. God provides for us first through the natural world God created; God is present and actively involved with every person we meet. Therefore, we must treat others with gentleness and respect, whether the other is a vulnerable child, a family on public assistance, a tyrant

---

[9] See John Wesley's sermon on 'The Means of Grace' in Albert Outler (ed.), *Bicentennial Edition of the Works of John Wesley I*, (Nashville, Abingdon, 1983); Ralph Underwood, *Pastoral Care and the Means of Grace* (Minneapolis, Augsburg/Fortress, 1993), and Suzanne Johnson, *Christian Spiritual Formation in the Church and Classroom* (Nashville, Abingdon, 1989), pp. 121-124.

with political power, or a grandiose, dictatorial 'wannabe' whose only power is to irritate. When we begin to recognize God working with us, we begin to know ourselves. We may begin to know our need for forgiveness and acceptance, or we may recognize latent creative gifts that God means for us to use. Again, in traditional language, we begin to know ourselves not only as sinners but also as persons made in the image of God. On the basis of that self-knowledge, we can, with God's help, correct our path so that we do not lose our way toward love and justice. This turning, or *metanoia*, Wesleyans call convicting and justifying grace.

As we turn, our eye searches for the path toward the love of God in heart, soul and mind, and the love of the neighbor as oneself. We anticipate that with God's help, we can continually find our way along, or back to, this path. This path, the way of salvation, always aims toward individual and social holiness, defined as promoting love and justice in individuals and society. If in our walk on this path we ignore individuals in order to promote some version of social progress, or we privatize religion into an individualized piety without attention to social justice, we have lost our way. For Wesleyans, the appearance of convicting and justifying grace in our lives always necessitate the presence of God's sanctifying grace, and we are fully responding to God's sanctifying grace only when individual and social holiness become an integrated whole in our lives. Therefore, a Wesleyan theologian must grapple with the uncomfortable ambiguity of hearing that 'the world is my parish'. I believe that I violate my Wesleyan theological beliefs if I construct the field of pastoral care so that some populations are systematically eliminated or if I narrow my consideration of the range of caring practices to one caring specialty or another. My Wesleyan beliefs call me to reflect on a wide range of ways of caring, and the social ecological structure of pastoral care helps to bring this breadth to life.

Wesleyan theology developed as a reflection on the caring practices of John and Charles Wesley. For John and Charles, Jesus' life of caring for the poor, the imprisoned, the uneducated, the despairing, the politically despised, and the spiritually seeking created a theological norm and ecclesial spirit by which the paths of church and society were to be judged. The Wesleys pursued the theological norm and ecclesial spirit of caring, even when it meant breaking church law to do so. Original Wesleyan theology, as found in the sermons, commentaries, diaries, prayers, and occasional writings of John Wesley and in the hymns of Charles Wesley, reflect the religious experience of the Wesleys as they and their followers acted upon this theological norm and ecclesial spirit.[10]

Wesleyan heritage offers a depth tradition of caring practice, among women and laity in addition to men and clergy. Long before the word 'feminism' was popularized, Wesleyan women cared for all humankind by preaching, teaching, and conducting class meetings; by ministering with the poor, the imprisoned, the violated, the sick; by challenging ecclesial and political structures of exclusion. Women reinterpreted scripture, organized sewing circles for the economic care of poor women and children, fought against violence, abuse, and organized prostitution, and organized schools to educate women in the United States and abroad. And, women explained what they were doing theologically, becoming practical theologians of the church along side the formally recognized academic theologians.

Studying the lives of historical women has been an act of care for my students and myself. By enlarging our knowledge of the women's tradition in which we stand and the women who formed that heritage, we relativize and depersonalize our present struggles. We discover that certain historical patterns pertain to women's lives, particularly within institutions. Frequently, Wesleyan and other women fought for causes that were not resolved in their own lifetime; like Moses, they died not knowing that their life's work would be rewarded in gains for the younger generation in a few short years. They also did not know how rapidly their

[10] See Pamela Couture, *Blessed Are the Poor? Women's Poverty, Family Policy, and Practical Theology* (Nashville, Abingdon, 1991) and Theodore Jennings, *Good News to the Poor: John Wesley's Evangelical Economics* (Nashville, Abingdon, 1990).

efforts could fade from public consciousness. Since many of our foremothers have sacrificed for women's present privileges, whether in church, society, or politics, theological virtue exists in appreciating those privileges and using them to contribute to the good of other human beings. When we seek to orient ourselves toward love and justice and we encounter frustrations, setbacks, and even genuine suffering, we can be strengthened by spiritual friendship with women we will never know who continue to care for us by the witness of their lives. Our foremothers remind us that while we should never seek suffering, we may at times be claimed to sacrifice for questions and causes that may not be resolved in our own lifetime. Learning and teaching the women's tradition in which we stand is a psychological and spiritual necessity, an act of care for women who allow their theological values to guide their path. [11]

The practical lens

The feminist and Wesleyan lenses already focus on practices, situations, and habits in the life of individuals, families, churches, societies, and governments. In feminist theology, women's experience is emphasized as a subject for reflection; in Wesleyan theology, religious experience is equally important. In some ways feminist and Wesleyan theologies[12] already qualify as practical theologies, although practical theology, as I understand it, is not exhausted by the content or methods of either feminist or Wesleyan theologies. Practical theology must begin and end in practice, both those practices that are ecclesial and those that are not.

---

[11] Rosemary Keller (ed.), *Spirituality and Social Responsibility: A Vocational Vision of Women in the United Methodist Tradition* (Nashville, Abingdon Press, 1993); see also Hilah F. Thomas and Rosemary Skinner Keller (eds.), *Women in New Worlds: Historical Perspectives on the Wesleyan Tradition I* (Nashville, Abingdon, 1981), and Rosemary Sinner Keller, Louise L. Queen, and Hilah F. Thomas, *Women in New Worlds: Historical Perspectives on the Wesleyan Tradition II* (Nashville, Abingdon, 1982).

[12] See Randy L. Maddox, *Responsible Grace: John Wesley's Practical Theology* (Nashville, Kingswood Books, 1994).

As Don Browning and Douglas Meeks have shown for psychology and economics, respectively, even so-called secular theories and practices implicitly proclaim a theology through their metaphors of ultimacy, visions of the human and divine, and the divine-human encounter.[13] Even experienced-focused feminist and Wesleyan theologians do not necessarily make explicit how their theology suggests specific practices.

As a practical theologian, I grow concerned about academic theology when it is understood as an end in itself rather than as a means for love and justice. I ask: Where are we academics constructing idols – in other words, unwittingly promoting visions of ultimacy which contradict our vision of the God we seek to follow? What is the purpose of theological specialties – Biblical studies, church history, ethics, systematic and practical theologies – if teachers cannot also integrate their specialities into an overall vision of ministry? What is the purpose of theological abstraction that cannot also be translated into the various languages of the faithful? In a world riddled with violence and poverty, can we afford the material and emotional resources that support theological thought projects if they do not contribute to a better world?

Practical theology is a critical theological discipline.[14] It assesses claims about who God is and who we are in light of the God in whom we claim to believe. It recognizes that claims for loyalty to competing and irreconcilable God-images may occur within theology or between theologies and various sciences. When differing God-images become evident in theology, a practical theologian should be prepared to interpret to the church and to the public the advantages and disadvantages of various God-images. In our critical task, however, we do well to heed Aristotle's warning regarding practical reason: 'Do not admit more precision to

    [13] Don S. Browning, *Religious Thought and the Modern Psychologies: A Critical Conversaton in the Theology of Culture* (Philadelphia, Fortress Press, 1987); and M. Douglas Meeks, *God the Economist* (Minneapolis, Fortress Press, 1989).
    [14] Don Browning, *A Fundamental Practical Theology: Descriptive and Strategic Proposals* (Minneapolis, Fortress Press, 1991).

the subject matter than the subject matter admits.'[15] Practical theology, while critical, is also tentative. It recognizes the plurality and ambiguity of the meanings that we attach to practices. Practical theology also increasingly recognizes that embodied practices, especially acts of ministry, form our sense of who we are and who God is in non-verbal ways.

Just as the family practitioner specializes in being the generalist of medicine, the practical theologian specializes in generalist theology. A practical theologian will not be schooled in the particularities of the theological specialties but must know when the knowledge of the specialties should be called upon. A practical theologian is a specialist in integrative theology. Reciprocally, today's theological specialist must learn the role of the generalist and must have a concept of how his or her specialized discipline is reintegrated into the general purposes of clergy and lay ministry as a whole.

In contrast to the theological specialist who predominantly writes for an elite audience, it is incumbent upon the practical theologian to write for a variety of audiences. The practical theologian must be multilingual, capable of writing and speaking for his or her academic peers, church leadership, non-church constituencies who are interested local faith communities, and theological seekers. The practical theologian must also be prepared to communicate in the non-verbal languages of the church: in the arts, in acts of liturgy, and in material and emotional care beyond words. Communicating in straightforward non-academic discourse without losing meaning is more difficult than writing and speaking in the jargon of one's immediate peers. A practical theologian must develop her linguistic versatility.

Finally, it is a dimension of the art of the practical theologian to discern the relationship between the pursuit of theological truth and mission, or service to the common good. How do we compare the good produced from the time, energy and money that we spend

---

[15] Aristotle, *Nicomachean Ethics I:3* in Richard McKeon (ed.), *Introduction to Aristotle* (Chicago, University of Chicago Press, 1973), p. 347.

in theological education and research with the good produced if we were to spend our time, energy and money directly in mission? How do we weigh, for example, the good produced by using an hour to gather data on the plight of children's poverty, to attend a committee meeting about a program for poor children, or to help a poor child with her homework? Too often, the pursuit of truth obscures the purpose of theology as a means to faith lived in a holy individual and social life. Conversely, our desire for efficiency and results can easily undermine our pursuit for truth. One aim of practical theology is to seek truth through lived faith.

Yet practical theology which pursues its truth by living it is often judged as unscholarly or unacademic. To demonstrate, why has no professor of religion ever won the Nobel Peace Prize? In many departments of great universities the presence of an array of Nobel Laureates is a sign of the university's academic excellence. And, one would think that actively promoting world peace would be high on the agenda of the world's greatest theologians. A review of Nobel Laureates reveals that professors in economics, political science, and philosophy have won the Peace prize. But in religion, activists, clergy, and religious organizations, not academics, have been deemed to make the greatest contributions to world peace. Promoting world peace in a significant way would require a professor to engage in lived practical theology. Academic scholarship in religion is not presently structured to reward significant practical theological engagement.

Academic theologians have worked since the late nineteenth century at legitimating theology in a world of science. For this purpose we have emulated the methods of science, even when scientific methods do not answer all theological questions. We have not necessarily adopted the best values of science, those which integrate the pursuit of truth and service to the common good, allowing them to undergird theologically-appropriate methods. Might practical theologians not be expected to raise questions which evaluate whether our means of theological study and learning adequately encourages lives turned toward the ultimate good of love and justice in God?

Picturing pastoral care

Let us look, for a moment, at pastoral care and social change through a 'wide-angled' lens. The practice of pastoral care, as we presently know it, grew from the religion and health movement which developed in response to the social change of the early twentieth century in the United States. At that time the United States was changing from being predominantly agrarian to becoming industrialized. The infectious diseases of an agrarian society gave way to the chronic diseases produced by industrial conditions. New discoveries in science, more sophisticated medical institutions, and a newly-organized medical profession rose to the challenge of treating those diseases. In the midst of these changes, ministers and doctors transformed pastoral care so that it could respond to, and proactively promote religion and spirituality in this new society. Clinical pastoral education and pastoral counseling were born.[16]

Western society is presently undergoing another major transition: from industrialization to a service-oriented, information-centered society. We are vulnerable to the diseases and social disorders wrought by this change.[17] Epidemiologist Alan Dever and his colleagues characterize the emerging diseases as stress and depression over outmoded skills, the need to learn new technologies for employment, and information overload. In particular, people are asked to make and be responsible for choices based on information beyond their ability to absorb. 'Information overload', they write, 'requires people to make endless choices among options, causing stress and eventually social shock. Nonetheless, restricting the opportunity for choice transforms the desire to choose into the 'need' to choose.'[18] And, the need to choose leads us increasingly to invest ultimate value in the belief that our most significant responsibility is choosing and choosing rightly.

[16] E. Brooks Holifield, *A History of Pastoral Care in America* (Nashville, Abingdon, 1983), pp. 175-258.
[17] G.E. Alan Dever, *Community Health Analysis: A Holistic Approach* (Germantown, Aspen Systems Corporation, 1980), pp. 1-30.
[18] Dever, *Community Health Analysis*, p. 13.

Dever categorizes the dys-eases of this disease cycle as psychological, lifestyle, genetic, and social. Although psychological problems result from many conditions, they are significantly associated with the use of illicit drugs, the onset of middle age, and the stresses of information overload. Lifestyle problems are defined as those which individuals could avoid by making different, albeit difficult, choices. In western societies, lifestyle problems are frequently associated with AIDS, lung cancer, and violence. Most significantly, violence is the fourth leading cause of death in the United States. Often, deaths from suicide, homicide, and automobile accidents can be traced back to drug and alcohol abuse. Genetic problems will result from the 'enormous risks and ethical dilemmas' of genetic mapping or engineering. While genetic discoveries have significant potential for the cure of disease, the unguided search for any knowledge and unbridled use of this knowledge could have 'cataclysmic results'. Finally, problems of social pathology arise when families and communities become inordinately unstable. Even positive social changes, such as more egalitarian gender and race relations, carry with them potential and actual conditions of insecurity in which new dys-eases can take hold. Taken together, these four conditions contribute to the diseases most likely to cause death and illness in the United States in the year 2000: diseases of the heart, cancer, cerebrovascular disease, accidents, AIDS, obesity/nutritional disorders, suicide, drugs/ alcoholism, aging/mental illness, coping/adaptability.

These stresses, according to Dever, will be aggravated as our society undergoes significant demographic change. The relatively low birth rate from 1929 to 1946 (due to the Great Depression and World War II) produced a generation who now, in later life, are able to experience relative abundance. In contrast, those who were born from 1946 to 1964, the 'Baby Boomers', can expect 'increasing frustration' as a well-populated generation enters its retirement years. As 'Baby Busters' reach childbearing age, the overall birth rate from 1995-2005 is anticipated to decline. Until about 2030, the fastest growing age group in the United States will be those over 65. After 2030, the population will grow faster among younger people.

Definitions of health have changed to meet the dys-ease of the society we are becoming. Rather than being understood in a narrowly biological sense, health is now considered to result from a number of social ecological factors: environment, lifestyle, biology, and systems of health care. According to the World Health Organization, 'Health is a state of complete physical, mental and social well-being and not merely the absence of disease and infirmity'. The concept of wellness moves even further toward a positive vision of health: wellness emphasizes physical activity, nutritional awareness, stress management, and self-responsibility. These new ways of thinking about health move in a similar direction to ways of thinking about care in a social ecological perspective. First, 'caring' involves creating a vision of fullness of life. Second, 'curing' disease or distress is an important but limited aspect of caring. Third, to care and cure we must understand the broad social, cultural, economic, political, and natural environment in which an individual or family lives. Appropriate care or cure may call for interventions at any or multiple levels of the social ecology in which a person lives. Finally, our caring with a person urges us to ask how we can mutually empower one another, not only to cure the ills of our lives, but to proactively create conditions for fullness of life.

To modify our approach to pastoral care in order to fulfill these commitments would be a complex task. I anticipate that we would continue to learn and teach others to do what pastoral care presently does well: assisting adults of the middle class who are associated with institutions, particularly hospitals, clinics, and churches, in times of life crises and transitions, illness, death, and suffering. We would continue to be the practice of ministry which is most concerned with the needs of individual persons while attending to the way that the individual is shaped by families, society, and culture. We would continue to stress the importance of empathic communication, adequate attention to human needs for attachment and separation, and basic principles of family and organizational systems. However, we would have to consider the care of individuals and families in relation to the care of society as a whole. We would have to think about care beyond adults of the middle class who are connected to institutions. A social ecological approach to pastoral care would draw on the whole range of experience and gifts that people bring to one another as they seek to care with one another in the presence of God. Caring would be about selecting and arranging what we have to offer to and receive from one another in a creative, imaginative expression of personal and divine presence – a genuinely artistic practice.

For example, in our changing society, child neglect and poverty is emerging as a dys-ease of epidemic proportions. In the United States one-fourth to one-third of the nation's children live in poverty. Poor children's lives are frequently marked by inadequate nutrition and health care and unsafe housing and schools. Children's psychic and social problems are developing earlier and with more severity. Children often get lost in families and community institutions. Poor and affluent children frequently share a similar deprivation: a poverty of relaxed time with adults, within and beyond the immediate biological family. Often, this problem is not the fault of parents; providing for a family stretches parents too thin. Proactive parenting now involves a complex coordination of influences, institutions, and professionals who become part of a child's life. Community and government services for children are frequently available, but parents may have difficulty getting information about services and application procedures can be burdensome. Even social service professionals find it difficult to know what services are available for children, who offers them, and how well they are evaluated. As almost a mirror image of the fragmentation of secular service, church programs for children exist, but churches find it difficult to get the right information about programs to the right people. In the transition away from a federal welfare system toward state welfare assistance, these problems and child poverty rates are expected to rise, at least for a while. In the meantime, something seems out of sync: the United States economy is flourishing.

Meaningful pastoral care with children and the poor involves interventions at all social ecological levels. It requires a spiritual and theological vision in which children are truly persons of God – persons to be listened to, who bring real concerns to the community of faith. It requires that church leaders be directly involved with individual children and with representing children's interests in programs and policies that change children's lives. It involves teaching adults to be concerned about the lives of children beyond their own immediate family, and it suggests that functional families need to assist struggling families to survive and thrive. Mentoring programs which connect individuals are important, and so are collaborative programs between neighborhood churches and community institutions. For example, experiments in which local churches have adopted neighborhood schools look promising. Similarly, church-state collaborations can be fruitful. In some cases, churches have adopted caseworkers who can call on the members of the church for support of all kinds for struggling children. In any case, meaningful pastoral care for children involves creating and promoting a theological vision of the church as one who lives for children in the 'spirit of adoption', holding various private and public organizations accountable for the values underwriting the policies of business and government. Furthermore, poor children of the United States are a witnessing presence, reminding us of children in dire, absolute poverty around the world. Such children are work of God's art. In pastoral care, we are called to be curators, ones who imagine ways to assist the public to safeguard their precious artwork for the future. Engaging purposefully in art requires vulnerability. Are we ready?

Becoming mid-wives to justice:
a feminist approach to practical theology

Carol Lakey HESS

> 'How can the differences that create our
> particular identities, differences of race,
> ethnicity, sexual orientation, class and
> gender, best be recognized, affirmed
> and understood?' Sharon Welch[1]

Introduction: practical theology as midwifery

Practical theology involves the process of shaping and enacting
a religious vision for life practice. Those engaged in practical theology draw upon theological tradition, cultural wisdom (including
the various sciences), religious practices, and the realities of life to
shape their vision. Different practical theologies give different
weight to the value of each of the contributing partners, but all
practical theologies engage each of the partners in some way or
other.[2] Practical theology is not, however, only an academic discipline; it is also a phenomenon rooted in communities of faith. In

---

[1] 'An Ethic of Solidarity and Difference', in Henry A. Giroux (ed.), *Postmodernism, Feminism, and Cultural Politics: Rethinking Educational Boundaries*
(New York, SUNY Press, 1991), p. 83.

[2] There are numerous methodologies for disciplined practical theologies;
broadly speaking, there are those which privilege the voice of one of the conversation partners (for example, theological tradition) and subordinate the others, and
there are those which attempt to hold the voices in equal balance. I place myself
in the last group. For one typology of practical theologies, see James N. Poling
and Donald E. Miller, *Foundations for a Practical Theology of Ministry*
(Nashville, Abingdon Press, 1985).

addition to the varieties of academic practical theologies, grass-roots forms of practical theology abound.[3] Confessing and practic-ing persons of faith bring theological convictions, cultural wis-dom, practical experience, and the realities of life to their religious expression. Sometimes they do this intentionally, other times it is more tacit; some of this theological reflection is thick and deep, other of it is more thin and on the surface. Thus, practical theology takes shape in critical and systematic forms and in habitual and ad hoc ways. 'As a theological discipline, practical theology repre-sents a more formalized version of the thinking process through which an average person attempts to bring social science, cultural traditions, and religious convictions into dialogue with one another,' remarks Pamela Couture.[4] One of the goals of this essay is to bring academic and grassroots practical theology into conver-sation, drawing both on a feminist approach to practical theology and women's practice in communities of faith. Theologian Carol Christ offers a 'feminist paradigm' for research and scholarship that assists me in accomplishing this goal.

A feminist methodology

Acknowledging that researchers bring to their work both a pas-sion for something particular and a willingness to learn from voices which stretch and modify that passion, Carol Christ con-structs an 'Ethos of Eros and Empathy' as a model for scholar-ship.[5] Drawing on women's interest in connection, Christ poses three 'moments' for scholarship: 1) naming the passion; 2) enlarg-

[3] I am indebted to Richard Osmer's vision of the three interlocking centers of the teaching office: academic, denominational, and congregational. See *A Teach-able Spirit: Recovering the Teaching Office in the Church* (Louisville, Westmin-ster/John Knox, 1990), Chapter 9.

[4] *Blessed Are The Poor? Women's Poverty, Family Policy, and Practical The-ology* (Nashville, Abingdon Press, 1991), p. 23.

[5] 'Toward a Paradigm Shift in the Academy and in Religious Studies', in C. Farnham (ed.), *The Impact of Feminist Research in the Academy* (Indianapolis, Indiana University Press, 1987).

ing the perspective; 3) exercising judgement. The first moment involves an awareness and articulation of the position of the scholar and the passion for transformation that drives the scholar's work.[6] The second moment is directed toward understanding the experience under research in a way that is empathetic to and enlarged by further study. The third moment involves a return to the now expanded standpoint, incorporating the insights gained. The researcher who is faithful to both Eros and empathy is confident in and committed to her passion but is also aware of her finitude and the provisional nature of its construction. She maintains her center and her voice, but she seeks out and learns from the perspectives of others.

In translating Christ's research model into a method for practical theology, I propose that the academic discipline of practical theology involves: the naming of the researcher's (research community's) location and guiding vision; the enlarging of that vision through observation of and participation in grassroots communal praxis; mutual judgement which both expands the vision and assists communities in realizing the vision. In the course of this essay, I will: 1) name my passion for 'communicative justice' in communities of faith and the greater public, 2) engage a particular group of women who groped toward something akin to my vision, 3) judge my vision in light of that engagement judgement and suggest how I might work as a midwife to further such a group's realization of the vision. Thus, in joining academic and grassroots theology, I have added Midwifery to Christ's last moment, the work of aiding communities beyond groping and toward realizing the nascent vision.[7] Midwifery is a tradition which involves acts of

---

[6] I have been much helped by Mary Elizabeth Mullino Moore, *Teaching From the Heart: Theology and Educational Method* (Minneapolis, Fortress Press, 1991).

[7] I have learned much from Don Browning's hermeneutical model of practical theology. Browning states that his efforts to think theologically about congregations is a conversation or dialogue in which I bring my questions and commitments to these congregations. In turn, I find myself confronted and questioned by their commitments and practices. See *A Fundamental Practical Theology: Descriptive and Strategic Proposals* (Minneapolis, Fortress Press, 1991), p. 15.

assistance and resistance. Like Shiprah and Puah (Exodus 1), mid-wives assist in birthing and resist killing those whom authorities quell because they are alien and threatening, in this case fledgling movements on the margins which threaten the status quo. Academic practical theology which learns from grassroots practical theology can serve as a mid-wife to communities who grope toward Spirit-breathed, justice-oriented, faith-inspired practice.

Research, theory, and location

Before offering the proposal for practical theology, it is important to make some remarks about the nature of passionate research. This essay is distinctively and self-consciously feminist. It draws on women's experience as a theoretical resource; it names the flourishing of women and men together as a theoretical purpose; and it consciously involves the location of the researcher as a part of the inquiry.[8] Furthermore, there is a feminist epistemology behind this work, reflected in both what I seek to know and how I think knowing occurs. Sandra Harding suggests that the 'questions an oppressed group wants answered are rarely requests for so-called pure truth. Instead, they are queries about how to change its conditions; how its world is shaped by forces beyond it how to win over, defeat, or neutralize those forces arrayed against its emancipation, growth, or development; and so forth'.[9] Conversation with others (with whom we differ with regard to religion, social/economic class, sex, race, culture or sexual orientation) is essential for knowing and overcoming of 'epistemological deficits' that result from an advantaged parochial vision.[10] 'All perspectives are partial and the creation of a moral vision and a strategy of moral action requires by definition the counterbalance of other groups and individuals,' argues Sharon Welch.[11] Welch goes so

---

[8] Sandra Harding, 'Is There a Feminist Method?', in Sandra Harding (ed.), *Feminism and Methodology* (Indianapolis, Indiana University Press, 1987).

[9] Harding, 'Is There a Feminist Method', p. 7.

[10] Harding, 'Is There a Feminist Method', p. 7.

[11] Sharon Welch, *A Feminist Ethic of Risk* (Minneapolis, Fortress Press, 1990), p. 38.

far as to claim that a single actor cannot be moral alone.[12] The fullness of knowing occurs in a conversational context where there is a fullness of participation in those seeking to know.

All theory and research reflects the class, race, culture, gender, history, and world view assumptions of the researcher. Although many theories and research findings are presented as if the theorist is invisible (and the findings universally applicable), the theorist is always deeply embedded in the analysis. Generally it is those theories from the margin that consciously mark themselves as perspectival, and thus it seems as if they are the only ones that are located. Practical interests, however, always inform theory. As feminist theorist Sandra Harding puts it,'The questions that are asked – and, even more significantly, those that are not asked – are at least as determinative of the adequacy of our total picture as are any answers that we can discover'.[13]

Recently, self-critical euro-American males have begun naming their location rather than claiming it to be 'unmarked' and thus universally valid. Biblical scholar Daniel Patte writes 'in and of themselves our male, European-American exegesis are and have always been contextual; they are thus 'interested', even though we contend that our use of rigorous critical methods ensures that they would be disinterested'.[14] This recognition of bias enables Patte both to critique and to claim the legitimacy of Euro-American contextual perspectives; he posits an androcritical interpretive stance which acknowledges pluralism, recognizes power and oppression, and remains accountable to others only by speaking with and not simply for and to others.

---

[12] The situation of the lone prophet, however, may be an indictment on community life. Thus, I express a corollary: the community which forces its dissenters to become single actors cannot be moral.

[13] Harding, 'Is There a Feminist Method', p. 7.

[14] Daniel Patte, 'Acknowledging the Contextual Character of Male, European-American Critical Exegesis: An Androcritical Perspective', in Fernando F. Segovia and Mary Ann Tolbert (eds.), *Reading from this Place*, vol. I: *Social Location and Biblical Interpretation in the United States* (Minneapolis, Fortress Press, 1995), pp. 35-56.

Although pure objectivism is impossible, when we reflexively engage our own subjectivity, we approach an honest objectivity, a genuine respect for the 'object' of our engagements. Freedom from subjective bias requires a naming of our history and an openness to the history of others. Objectivity, according to Beverly Harrison, 'means openness to others' history and to the critical claims that history bears and also the ability to learn from others' historical experiences'.[15]

The passion that drives my work, a commitment to justice, begins with the personal experience of suffering that results from difference. I am a daughter of the Holocaust; my Jewish mother (a native German) is the sole survivor of her immediate family. I am a more distant daughter of the Trail of Tears; my great-grandmother on my father's side was full Cherokee. In my history, the oppression that results from fear of otherness has many names – I share two women's names: Emy Pollack Schlösser (my murdered Jewish grandmother) and Elizabeth Roper (my 'relocated' Cherokee great-grandmother). It is increasingly my call and duty to point out that Emy's blood is not only on the hands of the evil Nazi Party that could not abide her differentness. The yellow stars that marked her as 'other' had their predecessors in Christendom's 'other fearing' anti-Jewish polemic which for centuries fueled the hatred and genocidal tendencies toward Jews.[16] The dehumanization of Elizabeth's people was motivated by racial, cultural, and religious imperialism; not incidently, the imposing white culture worked to quench the striking woman-centered ways of Native American peoples. Although I emerged out of the poverty of my childhood by assimilating to the dominant cultural norm, it is with a sense of triumph that I recover the 'red roots of white feminism'.[17]

---

[15] Beverly Wildung Harrison, *Making the Connections: Essays in Feminist Social Ethics*, ed. Carol S. Robb (Boston, Beacon Press, 1985).

[16] See for example Franklin H. Littell, *The Crucifixion of the Jews: The Failure of Christians to Understand the Jewish Experience* (San Francisco, Harper & Row, 1975).

[17] See Paula Gunn Allen, *The Sacred Hoop: Recovering the Feminine in American Indian Traditions* (Boston, Beacon Press, 1986).

My history energizes a theological and political passion for justice. Justice, which includes the defeat of oppressive forces, involves recognizing, engaging, and dispersing power among those who differ from one another. Following the above named methodology for midwifery, moving from passion to empathy to judgement, I will now elaborate the body of my proposal for practical theology.

Naming the passion: communicative justice

Justice begins with recognizing, affirming, and understanding differentness. This has been a crucial aspect of feminism in its varieties. '[T]he affirmation of diversity and multiplicity in feminist theology is based on our beliefs that gender is historically conditioned. There is not an 'abstract' woman, nor is there an 'abstract' man,' notes Kwok Pui-Lan.[18] Feminisms arose as prophetic critiques of the way in which a male dominated world made into 'other' and oppressed the differentness of women. Still, early expressions of feminism had to come to grips with their own differentness – and repent of their own forms of imperialism. Originally a movement composed of white privileged women, feminism has been called to task by women who contend that racism, classism, and heterosexism must be faced – within as well as without feminism – in addition to sexism.[19]

Justice also entails the engagement of difference; intentional conversation (and not merely toleration) must take place. Those who attempt conversation speak and listen to one another, questioning and probing back and forth. They seek to highlight their particularity while at the same time understand one another, both being distinctive 'other', and being willing to be changed by and

---

[18] 'The Future of Feminist Theology: An Asian Perspective', in Ursula King (ed.), *Feminist Theology from the Third World* (Maryknoll, Orbis Books, 1994), p. 66.
[19] See Audre Lorde, *Sister Outsider* (Freedom, California, The Crossing Press, 1984), pp. 66-71.

to disagree with one another. Most importantly, they mutually shape the nature and direction of their communication together. Though celebration of difference is an appropriate part of conversation, authentic conversation is not a 'tourist's delight' where surface sharing takes place. 'Real conversation that highlights difference entails clash and conflict'.[20] When we 'celebrate' differentness, we must be aware that the exhilaration that can come from engaging others is often on the other side of pain and struggle.

Finally, justice involves the dispersing of power. Iris Marion Young, in her important book *Justice and the Politics of Difference*, contrasts a paradigm of 'distributive justice' with one of 'communicative justice'. 'The distributive paradigm defines social justice as the morally proper distribution of social benefits and burdens among society's members'.[21] Some groups have social goods which others lack; distributive justice works out the best way to allocate goods more equitably. There is much merit in this view, but as a paradigm for justice it is incomplete. The distributive paradigm often fails to take into account the 'justice of decision making power and procedures'. Sharing goods is benevolent, but sharing the power for making decisions, defining culture, and shaping procedures is much more important. Those who share the goods they themselves value while holding onto the right to determine what is good still exercise domination over those toward whom they are benevolent. For example, we can make sure that every person in our community is served supper every night, given adequate clothing to wear, and supplied with a house to keep them warm. This is distributive justice. Benevolent and charitable though it is, it generally falls short of full justice. If only one group determines the menu, selects the fashion styles, and draws up the blue-prints for the house, then communicative justice, the 'justice of decision making power and procedures', is lacking for the other groups.

[20] Mark Kline Taylor, *Remembering Esperanza: A Cultural-Political Theology for North American Praxis* (Maryknoll, New York, Orbis Books, 1990), p. 62.
[21] Iris Young, *Justice and the Politics of Difference* (Princeton, Princeton University Press, 1990), p. 16.

Self-respect, a good that cannot be allocated, is highly dependent on cultural definitions of what is worthy. If a person feels that they are validated by and able to shape the direction of the wider culture, they are more likely to have self-respect. If, however, decisions are being made and culture is being defined apart from their contributions, then they have little social/cultural power and are marginated.[22] The caring leader who only 'communicates' her vision of justice or only 'distributes' the goods already prescribed is still missing the 'communicative' dimension of justice. Communicative justice would aim toward processes and procedures which disperse social/cultural power among all groups of persons. The scope of justice, then, is wider than the distribution of goods. Communicative justice requires a fair discussion of and argument over the future of a social group. Communicative justice demands that we not simply distribute food, clothing, and shelter but we empower many groups to take part in the discussion over menu, clothing styles, and architecture.

Thus, communicative justice engages the varieties of difference within the community. Difference is not merely something to tolerate; the interplay of differentness foments creativity and vitality. So often we are taught either to ignore difference (and thus maintain a shallow relationship) or to change those who are different (and thus create an oppressive relationship). 'Difference must be not merely tolerated, but seen as a fund of necessary polarities between which our creativity can spark like dialectic,' asserts Audre Lorde. This courageous encounter with difference fosters

---

[22] Pierre Bourdieu's theory of *cultural capital* is helpful here. Bourdieu contends that schools determine what knowledge (both in terms of content and form) has greatest worth, and they tend to reflect the knowledge and values of dominant groups in many societies, thus validating and reinforcing those values. This not only reinforces that which students from the dominant culture bring from home (and thus advantaging them), it also renders other groups and culture invisible. Students will intuit that what is not taught is not worthy of learning, and the history, contributions, and values of cultures other than the dominant one will not be considered to constitute legitimate knowledge. Bourdieu contends that this is *symbolic violence* against cultures and groups that are devalued. See Pierre Bourdieu, 'The forms of Capital' in John G. Richardson (ed.), *Handbook of Theory and Research for the Sociology of Education* (New York, Greenwood Press, 1986).

an understanding of interdependence that is unthreatening. 'Only within that interdependency of different strengths, acknowledged and equal, can the power to seek new ways of being in the world generate, as well as the courage and sustenance to act where there are no charters,' remarks Lorde.[23]

Distributive justice entails teaching people how to get along in present power structures; in the North American context, distributive justice is passing on 'street smarts' for democratic living. Communicative justice is not simply teaching people to adapt (play the master's game); it is also building on the skills, powers, experience, knowledge, and talents that people have which are unacknowledged in the power structures (so they can reshape the master's game). People who use non-mainstream forms of communication do not have equal power and thus do not always feel safe expressing themselves in community, and they therefore are kept from the central formative power of community life. Communicative justice requires inviting such people to shape a community's life not simply by rational discourse, but also by storytelling, spiritual expression and 'God-talk',[24] dance, song and music of all kinds, drama, folk and classic art, poetry, meditation, prayer, encounters with nature, anger, defiant speech, wrenching lament, mourning, weeping, silence, and more.

Dynamic difference in communion

While my sensitivity to difference and otherness emerges out of the particularities of my personal history as Jew/Cherokee/woman/other, it also grows out of my understanding and dwelling in the 'depth grammar' of a Trinitarian God. Recognizing, affirming, and

---

[23] Lorde, *Sister Outsider*, p. 111.

[24] Joanna Bowen Gillespie, who interviewed 'ordinary women in a mainline denomination', borrows this expression from one of her interviewees who boldly announced what it is she wanted from church: 'I want real God-talk'. *Women Speak: Of God, Congregations and Change* (Valley Forge, Pennsylvania, Trinity Press International, 1995), p. 2.

understanding differentness is central to the God who created the world, was incarnate in a human being, and is present through the power of the Spirit. 'God is self-sharing, other-regarding, community-forming love,' sums Daniel Migliore. Migliore claims that this is the 'depth grammar' of the doctrine of the Trinity, which 'lies beneath all the 'surface grammar' and all the particular, and always inadequate, names and images that we employ when we speak of the God of the gospel'.[25] The triune God is not only understood to be a union of diversity, but the triune God is inextricably connected and related to the differentness of created life.[26]

According to Catholic theologian Catherine La Cugna, 'the doctrine of Trinity is ultimately a practical doctrine with radical implications for Christian life'.[27] Recovering and reappropriating the tradition of the Cappadocians, LaCugna emphasizes that it is God's fundamental nature to be in relation. 'The ultimate source of all reality is not a 'by itself' or an 'in itself' but a person, a toward-another,' she insists. God's relationality is material and incarnate; the trinity affirms God's active participation in human life. Rather than being contented to live within an absolute oneness, God enters the messiness of life in relation with those who are different.[28] Relationality, then, is 'at the heart of God's essence … Personal interrelationship indicates the manner of God's rela-

[25] Dan Migliore, *Faith Seeking Understanding* (Grand Rapids, Michigan, Eerdmans, 1991), p. 64.

[26] Unfortunately an understanding of the Trinitarian Christian God was all but abandoned in the development of Christian thought during the expansion and consolidation of imperial Rome. God's power, understood as God's control, was seen as dependent upon God's unity, which, as Susan Thistlethwaite puts it, was 'threatened even by sharing with Godhead itself'. See 'I Am Become Death: God in the Nuclear Age', in Susan Brooks Thistlethwaite and Mary Potter Engel (eds.), *Lift Every Voice: Constructing Christian Theologies from the Underside* (San Francisco, HarperCollins, 1990), p. 99.

[27] La Cugna, *God For Us: The Trinity and Christian Life* (San Francisco, HarperCollins, 1973), p. 250.

[28] La Cugna makes the controversial claim that we must not separate the immanent trinity of speculation from the economic trinity of experience. When we speculate about God's relations within the godhead, separate from God's activity in human life, we forget the fact that the God we know is God with us, a God who chose the messiness of incarnation, and not God within Godself.

tionship with the world, and diversity among divine persons is a
principle for affirmation of the diversity within creation'.[29]

The Hebrew understanding of a dynamic God in relationship
with humanity, and the Christian understanding of a God whose
unity embraces diversity, call forth a communion of others that
overcomes alienation while preserving particularity.[30] It is an
interdependent community where knowledge and truth are not
simply asserted but discovered in the interaction of differences, a
'communion that abolishes solitariness but not individuality'.[31]
Furthermore, it is not a community of mere tolerance, but rather a
dynamic and even conflicted engagement with sometimes painful
difference. References to the Spirit of God are often typified as
communion bringing unity; the presence and activity of the Spirit
of God actually points to the gathering, interaction, and interdependence of those with differences. While the highly idealized
version of mellifluous community life in Acts 4 is deeply embedded in our imaginations, this is neither a possible nor a desirable
paradigm for day to day living in community. Acts 15, with its
portrayal of hard debate, dissension, disagreement, mutual listening, and attentiveness to new possibilities is far more fitting and
liberating. It is this kind of community that gropes toward genuine
justice; such justice, however, is hard won.

A post-modern discourse ethic

One of the reasons that visions of harmonious community life
are so compelling is that we are in a time of serious social and
psychological fragmentation. This has caused us to yearn for 'the
ideal of community'. Such a yearning is understandable, but theologically and politically problematic.'Those motivated by [this

---

[29] La Cugna, *God For Us,* p. 264.
[30] See James E. Loder and W. Jim Neidhardt, *The Knight's Move: The Relational Logic of the Spirit in Theology and Science* (Colorado Springs, Helmers &
Howard, 1992).
[31] La Cugna, *God For Us, p.* 298.

yearning for ideal community] will tend to suppress differences among themselves or implicitly to exclude from their political [and religious, CLH] groups persons with whom they do not identify'.[32] Communitarian theorists argue for cohesive community life with a shared set of principles and values; ideological groups seek unity and wholeness, looking for mutual identification and affirmation. The danger for communitarians and ideological communities is that these groups become closed to 'unassimilated otherness', and thereby suppress conflict in their midst and reproduce homogeneity.

In order to achieve communicative justice, a purpose which emerges from a response to the depth grammar of a trinitarian God, communities of faith will need to recognize, engage, and empower differentness. In the word of contemporary philosophy, we will need to live according to a post-modern 'discourse ethic'. By discourse ethic, I mean an approach to community life that involves intense conversation and argumentation over formative practices and decisions. By post-modern, I mean that it draws on the insights of the modern universalist tradition without buying into the metaphysical illusions of the enlightenment.

This vision of discourse ethics originates with Jürgen Habermas, who has labored to finish the unfilled project of modernity – to provide a better future for all members of society based on rational knowledge. Habermas contends that 'ideal' conditions for speech are possible. Recognizing the problems of conflicting interests and ideological taint in communication, he offers a complex theory of 'undistorted communication', which supplies norms for reasonable and valid discourse amongst different parties.[33] The competencies required for undistorted communication are: to

---

[32] Iris Young, 'The Ideal of Community and the Politics of Difference', in Linda J. Nicholson, *Feminism/Postmodernism* (New York, Routledge, 1990), p. 300.

[33] See J. Habermas, *Communication and the Evolution of Society* (Boston, Beacon Press, 1979), p. 3. The following discussion is indebted to Richard J. Bernstein (ed.), *Habermas and Modernity* (Cambridge, MA, The MIT Press, 1985).

make factual claims about things in the world which can be tested by experience, to say things which will help regulate our interpersonal relations, and to express oneself and one's intentions authentically. Habermas' basic assumption is that communication inherently requires the capacity to give good reasons for our actions and beliefs, reasons that make sense even to those who do not share our presuppositions. While fully aware of the limitations of the Enlightenment, Habermas seeks to defend and reconstruct its emancipatory aspirations, pressing for the autonomy and freedom of all human subjects.[34] Furthermore, he believes that if all persons seeking truth engage in genuine communication and open to the 'force of the better argument', they can reach consensus concerning what is right. The 'core idea' behind this theory of 'communicative ethics' is: 'namely the processual generation of reasonable agreement about moral principles via an open-ended moral conversation'.[35]

A post-modern discourse ethic retains the 'core idea' of including all persons in argumentation without claiming that there is a self-transparent and self-grounding reason that is situated beyond historical and cultural contingency.[36] Seyla Benhabib argues that 'the fairness of moral norms and the integrity of moral values can only be established via a process of practical argumentation, which allows its participants full equality in initiative and continuing the debate and suggesting new subject matters for conversation'.[37] I would add that this process also allows its participation to initiate and validate alternative ways of knowing. A post-modern

---

[34] A number of practical and political theologians find Habermas' idea of communicative practice helpful to their work. See for example Helmut Peukert, *Science, Action, and Fundamental Theology: Toward a Theology of Communicative Action* (Cambridge, MA, MIT Press, 1984); Dennis P. McCann and Charles R. Strain, *Polity and Praxis: A Program for American Practical Theology* (Minneapolis, Winston Press, 1985).

[35] Seyla Benhabib, *Situating the Self: Gender, Community and Postmodernism in Contemporary Ethics* (New York, Routledge, 1992), p. 37.

[36] For a helpful analysis and critique see also Richard J. Bernstein, *Beyond Objectivism and Relativism: Science, Hermeneutics, and Praxis* (Philadelphia, University of Pennsylvania Press, 1983), pp. 171-230.

[37] Benhabib, *Situating the Self*, p. 73.

discourse ethic is committed to universal participation, and it intentionally expands the number of voices and a variety of forms of knowing in its moral and religious deliberations.

Habermas is critiqued by many for not providing a fully post-modern or genuinely liberating discourse ethic. Surely, his insistence upon the norm of a good argument rather than the compulsion of tradition or the exertion of power provides a 'court of appeal' against obvious forms of duress and oppression. This norm itself, however, fails to provide for alternative modes of conversation. Habermas thus depreciates cultural traditions that are different from the Western intellectual tradition. Modern culture, in his view (indebted to Piagetian theory of cognitive development), is more 'cognitively adequate' than cultures steeped in myth or primitive world views – which operate at a 'lower level of rationality'.[38] Strikingly, in his work *Theory of Communicative Action*,[39] Habermas summarily dismisses the insights of oral cultures. He works hard to extend Western rationality to others but does not as adequately seek to redefine conversation in light of others. While Habermas' theory is aimed to overcome inequalities in discourse by positing a theory of just communication, in the end he creates conditions for conversation that end in 'conquest' of others.[40]

Feminist educator Elizabeth Ellsworth argues that 'dialogue' is not always empowering for the intended participants if the process of dialogue is predetermined by an advantaged group.[41] A justice-

[38] For a discussion of the mutually validating relationship between his discourse theory of ethics and Lawrence Kohlberg's (Piagetian based) theory of the development of moral consciousness, see Habermas' essay 'Moral Consciousness and Communicative Action', in his book by the same title, translated by Christian Lenhardt and Shierry Weber Nicholsen with an introduction by Thomas McCarthy (Cambridge, MA, MIT Press, 1990), pp. 116-194.

[39] *Volume One: Reason and the Rationalization of Society* (Boston, Beacon Press, 1984 ET); *Volume Two: System and Lifeworld* (Boston, Beacon Press, 1988 ET).

[40] See Anthony Giddens, 'Reasons Without Revolution?', in Richard J. Bernstein (ed.), *Habermas and Modernity* (Cambridge, MA, MIT Press, 1985).

[41] 'Why Doesn't this Feel Empowering? Working Through the Repressive Myths of Critical Pedagogy', in Carmen Luke and Jennifer Gore (eds.), *Feminisms and Critical Pedagogy* (New York, Routledge, 1992).

seeking discourse ethic deems it particularly important to grant
some privilege to the views and ways of knowing of those who
have traditionally been excluded from public discourse. Those we
have excluded from the interpretive community are necessary for
the experience of truth; and a genuine discourse ethic draws on the
varieties of people to shape the future of a community.[42] When it
is not possible or desirable to include outsiders within one's community, it is important for different community's to engage one
another.[43]

Justice in conversation is not merely a social goal in response to
shifting demographics; it is an ethical and epistemological commitment to fight oppression and mobilize differentness on the way
to knowing.[44] This means that assimilation cannot be the primary
goal, but rather reciprocity. Even if we do not come to a common
agreement with the others with whom we enter into dialogue, we
come out of such an encounter with a better understanding of the
partiality, limits, and also the value of our own positions.[45]

[42] For instance, a white male understanding of God's providence comes with a
pervasive experience of control and privilege. White males are responsive and
effective and get things done; white male Gods are powerful, in control, and
effective in accomplishing their will. Not only is this a selective reading of the tradition, but it is also an isolated encounter with the tradition.

[43] Here a caveat is necessary. While dominant groups need to diversify, mar-
ginal groups may need to join in solidarity; the former must not be at the expense
of the latter. Many dominant groups 'diversify' by assimilating others to the dominant pattern. This is not genuine diversification. Those who belong to dominant
groups need to critically assess assimilative procedures, and they need to guard
against breaking up communities of solidarity in order to achieve their diversify-
ing ends.

[44] Multi-culturalism is an ambiguous process; sometimes issuing in the dominant culture being enriched once more by raiding other cultures of their treasures.
While this does not mean that multi-culturalism is to be disregarded, it does mean
that we need to make it a multi-culturalism of political life (affecting decision-
making) and not simply a smörgåsbord of cultural artifacts. See Sonia Nieto,
Affirming Diversity: The Sociopolitical Context for Multicultural Education, 2nd
edn (White Plains, New York, Longman Publishers, 1996).

[45] This is a departure from Habermas who feels that consensus based on
mutual assessment of the validity of the arguments is the goal of genuine conversation. The press for consensus can perpetuate domination, and it can only
fall prey to an ethic of control that seeks to obliterate messiness and disagreement.

This understanding of discourse, while decidedly post-conventional (promoting critical reflection on the assumptions of one's tradition), is not anti-tradition. In a post-modern discourse ethic, tradition is a valued, even privileged voice in conversational discourse;[46] traditionalism (reducing and rigidifying tradition) is opposed, for it destroys conversation and slays its participants. Genuine discourse reactivates the variety of arguments present (but often reduced or harmonized) from the past of tradition and also engages with different and rival interpreters in the present.[47]

A discourse ethic is for the purpose of genuine justice and not simply for the imperialistic enrichment of those at the center – the center should shift as a result of genuine pluralism and engaged difference.

Enlarging the perspective with empathy: critical conversation with grassroots communities

Through the lenses of my passion,[48] I offer a brief 'qualitative' analysis of a woman's group, representing vital gropings toward

---

[46] Paula Gunn Allen exposes the colonial ideal that 'the best and the brightest should willingly reject and repudiate their origins' and thus forget their history and culture as quickly as possible. She argues that recovery of one's culture and traditions is critically important for oppressed persons. See *Sacred Hoop*, pp. 210-215.

[47] Mark K. Taylor describes the importance of both 'diachronic' (searching the past horizon of tradition) and 'synchronic' (engaging different cultural and political horizons in the present) strategies of interpretation. See 'Celebrating Difference, Resisting Domination: The Need for Synchronic Strategies in Theological Education', in Barbara Wheeler and Edward Farley (eds.), *Shifting Boundaries: Contextual Approaches to the Struggle of Theological Education* (Louisville, Westminster/John Knox, 1991).

[48] Good observation, according to Eliot Eisner, paints a picture that brings others into the reality described. This kind of observation is like a conversation, for it requires active listening and attentiveness to subtle cues and expressions; it moves in a dialogical manner, the observation process itself being shaped by that which is observed. While this kind of 'qualitative analysis' is different from 'quantitative analysis' which gathers statistical and numerical data according to a predetermined method, it is no less 'objective', for all empirical research is determined by the questions and lenses of the researcher. See Eisner, *The Enlightened Eye: Qualitative Inquiry and the Enhancement of Educational Practice* (New York, Macmillan, 1991).

justice. Women have long engaged in theological reflection and practice at the margins of community life. Though woman have not been major participants in academic practical theology, in many North American congregations, they constitute the majority of church members.[49] Thus, it is not only fitting to a feminist perspective on practical theology to look at women's theological reflection in communities of faith, it is also fitting to the make-up of the church.

Women at the grassroots groping toward justice

Many years ago, I served as a minister of education in a fairly affluent and well-educated congregation located in a secluded suburb. Though the town was bordered by a large, crime-ridden city on one side and several small, industrial working class communities on the other sides, it had the feel of being a haven in a troubled world. Many of the young families who moved there chose this borough for its safe ambiance. One of my most important responsibilities was pastoring church school teachers. In response to one women's request, I began a Bible study/prayer group for the teachers. Although there were a handful of male teachers, those who attended this group were all women. The women were all Caucasian, but they were economically and socially diverse. Several of the women were economically stressed, and a few others were dealing with severe emotional and/or mental trauma.

Jane was a participant in this weekly group. In addition to the Bible study, Jane was also involved in a prison ministry. Every week she joined a small cadre of folk who visited a women's

<hr>

[49] There is a body of literature discussing what is controversially known as 'the feminization' of North American religion. See Harry S. Stout and Catherine Brekus, 'A New England Congregation: Center Church, New Haven, 1638-1989', for a discussion of how this national trend was evident in a particular congregation. In James P. Wind and James W. Lewis, *American Congregations*, vol.1: *Portraits of Twelve Religious Communities* (Chicago, University of Chicago Press, 1994), pp. 14-102; esp 40-46. See also endnotes 46-59 in Strout and Brekus for further bibliography on the discussion surrounding this issue.

prison. A big part of the prison visitation group's mission was to bring craft projects for the women prisoners; they also brought conversation, Bible study, and prayer.

Jane's involvement with the prison ministry became part of the Bible study. At first she 'brought the prison' (so to speak) to the Bible study group by asking for donations, bringing Christmas packages to wrap, and sharing general concerns in prayer. Then she 'brought the prisoners' to the group by way of narrative; she told their stories and expressed her personal involvement with their lives. She also began to struggle openly with both her fear and even her revulsion toward these 'criminals' and her simultaneous sympathy and even sense of common humanity toward these women. She brought Angie, her favorite, a surprisingly gentle soul who in desperation and drunkenness had killed her abusive husband. She brought Suzanne, Corinne, and Donna who were transformed from in-mates in cells to persons with stories and even faces. We heard about poverty, racism, helplessness, violence, abuse, prostitution, homelessness, and abandonment. We saw glimmers of strength, determination, faith, hope and love in the midst of hopelessness and recidivism.

Finally, Jane 'brought the group' to the prison. I began visiting the prison, and the lives of the women prisoners became an integral part of the Bible study group's life. People didn't just add Angie to their prayer list, they also asked about her regularly. They didn't just think about Corinne at prayer time, they thought about her when they were interpreting the Bible passage. The lives of the women in prison became 'voices', strikingly 'other' voices, as these women gathered to hear and study the scripture together. The context for interpreting the Bible was changed; to be heard, the word of God had to make sense for and of Angie's life as well as for Jane's life. Sometimes lament, prayer, weeping, and silence were the only appropriate languages. The women began to ask questions of God and their theologies that they never asked before.

To varying degrees, this began a process of enlarging the group's notion of both Christian community and humanity. In the walls of the haven, windows and even doors to the outside were being constructed. Most group members were able to make the transition from thinking of the women as 'inmates' to be ignored to considering them 'sisters in God's love' with whom to minister. The ministry to this prison group became a ministry from the group as well. The group started to reflect on the way in which both privilege and deprivation chart the course of lives; we started to hear the hopelessness and helplessness of those whose destiny was wrought by the latter. We tried to hold in tension our awareness of 'sin' and seeming bad choices with compassion for the 'sinner' and understanding of the origin of those choices; and we made strides toward recognizing our own need of the grace that became more tangible and central to our lives. We cried to God for the pain experienced and caused by these women, and we cried to God for the pain we felt as their voices intruded upon our quiet world.

Certainly there were vestiges of an 'us-they' dichotomy between the two worlds, and the windows and doors never brought the walls tumbling down. But the group's world had been irrevocably enlarged beyond its original, somewhat provincial family centeredness. Most strikingly, the group moved toward embracing its own marginalized members and its own hidden brokenness. A schizophrenic member whose disruptiveness bothered the group was perceived with new eyes; and not only as one to whom to minister but also as one who brought gifts. The sharing of mutual concerns and need became ritualized. Group members were repeatedly mobilized both to seek care from one another and to offer care to one another. Facades of perfection began to be lifted as honest sharing took place. In opening to these 'strangers' in prison, members in the group also recognized the strangers within the group itself as well as the strangeness within each member.

It is important to note that a dual move was made by the women. They sought to understand how the gospel message could speak to the women in prison; they also began to interpret the biblical texts in light of the realities of imprisoned and impoverished women. It was not merely an imposition of the gospel upon the

women in prison; it was an openness to the women in prison illu-
minating the gospel.

These women were groping towards an enlarged mentality and
a just conversation with those who were different. Furthermore,
they were practical theologians seeking to weave together theology, social critique, religious practice, and life experience. This
women's group was engaged in a vital, justice-seeking practice,
groping practice showing promise for renewal of these women's
lives – and for the community at large.

Mutual judgement: expanding the passion and becoming a midwife to just community life

As noted above, the task of practical theology during this third
moment of research is a two-fold exercise of judgement: in order
to expand the original passion based on empathy with the sources
studied (eg. grass-roots practical theology) and in order to promote
the revised vision within the congregational setting.

This community of women helps us probe more fully the
concern raised by Iris Young concerning the 'ideal of community'. There was an interplay between the differences within
this group and the openness of this group to the women prisoners. The fact that the women already had marginalized ones in
their midst helped prepare them for their engagement with
those outside their bounds; conversely, their engagement outside their bounds enabled greater attentiveness to difference in
their midst.

In reflecting on this spiraling politics of difference, I was
prompted to expand my understanding of justice by making a distinction between a 'community of solidarity' and a 'life-style
enclave'. Life-style enclaves were denounced by Robert Bellah
and his associates in *Habits of the Heart* for being 'segmental'
groupings which celebrate the 'narcissism of similarity'. Such
enclaves 'involve only a segment of each individual, for they concern only private life, especially leisure and consumption. And

they are segmental socially in that they include only those with a common life-style'.[50] As opposed to genuine 'community' which attempts 'to be an inclusive whole' celebrating a variety of lifestyles, enclaves are comfortable and protected gatherings of the like-minded who prefer not to be in the company of those who do not share the same lifestyle. Communities of solidarity, however, are sometimes needed. These are gatherings of persons who share a common oppression, who protest against that oppression, and who attempt to construct alternative understandings of themselves as human beings.[51] 'Oppressed groups need to have separate spaces in which to gain their self-respect, name themselves, and discover their own history,' argues Davida Alperin.[52] Rather than an escape into private leisure, the goal of these communities is the empowering of oppressed persons for life in a public sphere which discriminates against them. This group of women helped me name what it is that prevents a community of solidarity from becoming a social enclave. Just as solidarity groups nurture the voices of those who speak out against domination, so too must they invite different voices within their own solidarity grouping. It is important that prophetic communities not become ideological strongholds, or else they become increasingly more like life-style enclaves. A leader helping a just community to be born will continually encourage it to attend to those on its own margins.

This experience compels me to be more patient with and tentative about my vision. As a visionary and an academic, I am tempted to foist my vision of justice upon communities. My understanding of justice was further enlarged by taking heed of the spontaneous and the gradual nature of what above is termed 'the

---

[50] Robert Bellah, et al., *Habits of the Heart* (Berkeley, University of California Press, 1985), p. 72.

[51] I have been greatly helped by Karla Ann Koll, 'Theology of Solidarity', in Philip E. Wheaton (ed.), *500 Years, Domination or Liberation? Theological Alternatives for the Americas in the 1990s*, (Ocean City, Md, Skipjack Press, 1992).

[52] Davida Alperin, 'Social Diversity and the Necessity of Alliances: A Feminist Perspective', in Lisa Albreach and Rose M. Brewer (eds.), *Bridges of Power: Women's Multicultural Alliances* (Philadelphia, New Society Publishers, 1990), p. 31.

spiraling politics of difference'. The movement of this group suggests that leaders do better to discern where approximations of their vision are struggling to be born. The connection between the women's group and the prison was not leader-initiated; it was supported and nurtured by the leader, but it came from within the group. Rather than guiding the women into this justice-groping ministry, the leader 'fanned into flames' a spark that emerged. The implication for community life is that a leader can foster her passion for justice in a community of faith by searching for spontaneous or fledgling ministries that can be encouraged toward the vision. This case also suggests that gradual movements toward enlarged perspectives can be sustained and furthered. As the group became more and more comfortable with their expanded discourse, the voices of those who were other played a larger and larger role in their reflection.

At the same time, this experience teaches me to look for moments when the birth of a more fully developed practice of justice is so imminent that it might be time to actively coach the people to work harder. Like a midwife who discerns the flow of events in a birth, I might have watched for the opportunity to tell this community it was time to 'push' and exert more focused effort on behalf of justice. This community of women did not go as far as they could toward realizing justice. As a distanced practical theologian, I see that I could have encouraged more advocacy on behalf of women in prison and helped to birth greater involvement in the prison itself. The central concerns of this group were expanded and even revised, but justice is still emerging. Just as Jane had brought the prison ministry to our attention, I might have informed the group about and involved the group in more 'hands on' kinds of activities.

SUMMARY

This model of practical theology uses an 'ethos of Eros, empathy and midwifery' which names its passion for genuine justice and goes in search of communities that are engaged in justice-seeking discourse and practice. The method has three moments: naming one's theological and political passion, enlarging the perspective through observation of and participation in grass-roots approximations of the passion, and exercising judgement both toward enlargement of the passion and toward assisting the community in furthering the passion. Academic practical theology, learning from grass-roots practical theology, can help draw out the processes already at work in communities of faith. Practical theologians can help leaders identify burgeoning movements toward justice so that they do not neglect them or kill them before they are born.

ADDITIONAL BIBLIOGRAPHY

Bordo, Susan. *Unbearable Weight: Feminism, Western Culture, and the Body*, Berkeley, University of California Press, 1993

Freire, Paulo and Ira Shor. *A Pedagogy For Liberation: Dialogues on Transforming Education*, New York, Bergin & Garvey, 1987

Hess, Carol Lakey. *Caretakers of our Common House: Women's Development in Communities of Faith*, Nashville, Abingdon Press, 1997

Hooks, Bell. *Talking Back: Thinking Feminist, Thinking Black*, Boston, South End Press, 1989

Neuger, Christie C. (ed.). *The Arts of Ministry: Feminist and Womanist Approaches*, Louisville, Westminster/John Knox Press, 1996

Nicholson, Linda J. *Feminism/Postmodernism*, New York, Routledge, 1990

Schipani, Daniel S. *Religious Education Encounters Liberation Theology*, Birmingham, AL, Religious Education Press, 1988

West, Cornel. *The American Evasion of Philosophy: A Genealogy of Pragmatism*, Madison, The University of Wisconsin Press, 1989

V

'A voice was heard in Ramah': a feminist theology of praxis for healing in South Africa

Denise ACKERMANN

Five fragments

'Thembinkosi's cries are still hurting me today. I want to know from the police where they took my children. Where did they kill my children?' Nohle Anna Nika-Jonas whose three sons, at the time all in high school, were taken from their shanty by police on the night of July 1, 1976.

'Just in pieces...pieces of him, brains, splattered all over the room'. Catherine Mlangeni describing how she found her son Bheki's body after he had been blown up by a police booby trap.

Joyce Mtimkulu, mother of Siphiwo killed by police, said she blamed former president F W de Klerk: 'He must have known about it. He must have known what was going on. I have always said it was the system. I still feel very sad. I have suffered for a long time and I want to see the men who killed Siphiwo'.

Cynthia Ngewu, mother of Christopher 'Rasta' Piet killed by police, said her notion of reconciliation was to 'restore the humanity of the perpetrators ... I don't want to replace one evil with another'.

Johan, a young, white, Afrikaner student of theology: 'My parents lied to me, my school lied to me, our leaders lied to me and the church lied to me. I don't even know the truth about God'.

Theology in a context of painful transition

The first four of the above fragments are extracts from evidence given by mothers of victims of the apartheid system before the Truth and Reconciliation Commission; the last fragment is from a conversation I had three years ago. These fragments are random flashes, moving pictures flitting across the screen of life in South Africa: truth-telling and truth-seeking, the need for justice and accountability, horror, pain and the shattering of illusions. Ours is a context of contrasts: of pain and hope, and the longing for a new day.

In April 1994 we experienced the miracle of a peaceful transition to democracy. We now have a new constitution with a bill of rights and a constitutional court to ensure that every citizen's rights are respected. We have commissions for human rights, for gender equity, for the interests of the youth. In May 1997, Tryphinah Mbele, aged 77, from Modderspruit village in the North West Province, became the one millionth person since 1994 to be supplied with water for the first time (*Sunday Times,* 4 May 1997). The air is full of concern for setting right former wrongs, for compensating those who formerly experienced racist discrimination and for social upliftment of the needy. All this was inconceivable only six years ago.

We are also grappling with the legacies of apartheid. Violence and criminality are placing the lives of many South Africans in a straitjacket of fear and uncertainty.[1] Poverty, displacement and ruptured family lives are still the social reality for scores of people. Violence against women, particularly rape and battering, has reached endemic proportions.[2] Diminishing resources are wreak-

---

[1] According to the World Health Organization, the incidence of violent death in South Africa-57 per 100,000 people – is now the highest in the world (*Cape Times,* 13 May, 1996).

[2] See Denise M. Ackermann, ''For such a thing is not done in Israel': violence against women' in L. Hulley, L. Kretzschmar and L. L. Pato (eds.), *Archbishop Tutu: Prophetic Witness in South Africa* (Cape Town, Human and Rousseau, 1996), pp.145-155 for a discussion on rape as a theological problem. See also Human Rights Watch/Africa, *Violence Against Women in South Africa: State Response to Domestic Violence and Rape* (New York, Human Rights Watch, 1995).

ing havoc with our systems of social security, education and health. It is difficult to translate the expectations of the majority of South Africans into concrete realities. We are a society suffering trauma, a society in transition.

While all the above facts are well known, a further deep concern is growing among members of religious communities. Evidence is mounting that the very leitmotifs which inspired the resistance to apartheid are being marginalised: issues of morality, values and ethics in the shaping of civil society. Theological education is a case in point. The teaching of theology at universities appears to be in jeopardy and seen as expendable in the push for technological proficiency. Does this imply that informed critical voices of religiously based communities are unwelcome in the new South Africa? If this is so what does it communicate about our leaders' visions for the future? What are the challenges to the church in this new situation?

Nowhere is the complex mixture of anguish, anger, anticipation and the search for truth and for an ethical foundation for our society more evident than in a unique process taking place at present in South Africa. As the Truth and Reconciliation Commission (set up in 1995) explores past violations of human rights, people of faith are challenged to wrestle with the meaning of grace, forgiveness, justice and reconciliation. By allowing victims to tell their tales of terror and torment, by considering requests for amnesty from perpetrators and by seeking reparation for victims, this venture hopes to root a culture of human rights in our country which will ensure that the suffering and injustices of the past will never occur again.[3] In the words of its chairperson, Archbishop *emeritus* Desmond Tutu, the commission 'remains a risky and delicate business, but it is still the only alternative to Nuremberg on the one hand and amnesia on the other' (*Sunday Times*, 8 December 1996).

[3] See H. Russel Botman and Robin M. Petersen, *To Remember and to Heal: Theological and Psychological Reflections on Truth and Reconciliation* (Cape Town, Human and Rousseau, 1996) for a collection of essays which reflect on the task of the Commission.

In this context I write as a white, middle-class woman, a member of the Anglican church, who teaches practical theology from a feminist perspective at an historically black university. In this article, I want to reflect critically from my place in my society on the contribution of a feminist theology of praxis to the healing of my country. After introductory remarks on a feminist theology of praxis, I shall consider the idea of healing as the core hermeneutic for such a theology. Various theoretical aspects of a feminist theology of praxis will be dealt with, followed by an attempt to explore their implementation in liberating and healing praxis for South Africa.

The events taking place before the Truth and Reconciliation Commission are the present boundaries within which I do theology. Why? I have not been ignorant of the ravages wrought by apartheid in the past. I have lost friends, lived through its scarring of my own family, heard the testimonies of my students and attempted to oppose it in my work and my life, often questioning the effectiveness of my actions and the consistency of my courage. Now, however, the all pervasive litany of suffering emerging from testimonies permeates my reality to such an extent that I am compelled to re-think the nature of my theological intentions. This is a time of anguished confrontation with naked bodily truth, a time of rupture and of new opportunities.

A feminist theology of praxis[4]

The dominant model for practical theology in South Africa emanates from a male, Reformed world. Not surprisingly my experience as a practical theologian has been one of writing and

---

[4] See Denise M. Ackermann, 'Engaging freedom: a contextual feminist theology of praxis', *Journal of Theology for Southern Africa,* 94 (March 1996), 32-49, for a more detailed description of such a theology as a 'critical, committed, constructive, collaborative and accountable reflection on the theories and praxis of struggle and hope for the mending of creation based on the stories and experiences of women/marginalized and oppressed people'.

speaking from the margins. It is a place which I have found lonely, challenging and rewarding. It has certainly been instructive about the relationship between theology and the power of social, political and educational structures within male-dominated frameworks.[5]

Feminist theologians, rather than working within the traditional confines of the theological encyclopedia, generally prefer to orient their theologies towards particular issues which are rooted in experience and illuminated by systemic analysis.[6] Stories which tell of the experiences of women, children and all marginalized and oppressed people raise issues which are sources for theorizing on liberation and healing. These issues enter into critical dialogue with reigning theological models, exposing inadequacies and biases and calling for the reconstruction of our practical theological discourse. A feminist theology of praxis which is critical of current models of practical theology for their inherent male-orientation and inability to deal with the reality of the lives of women, children and the poor, reflects on the experiences of the 'others' in order to act collaboratively with them for a transformed world.

Trained as a practical theologian, I am familiar with the different approaches to our subject and the richness of its field of study.[7]

---

[5] During the apartheid era, the white Dutch Reformed Church, the *de facto* state church of white minority Nationalist party rule, trained its ministers (in practical theology) in seminaries and faculties at state funded universities.

[6] I refer here, *inter alia*, to the work of the following feminist practical theologians: Riet Bons-Storm, *The Incredible Woman: Listening to Women's Silences in Pastoral Care and Counselling* (Nashville, Abingdon Press, 1996); Pamela D. Couture, *Blessed are the Poor? Women's Poverty, Family Policy and Practical Theology* (Nashville, Abingdon Press, 1991); Nancy L. Eiesland, *The Disabled God: Toward a Liberatory Theology of Disability* (Nashville, Abingdon Press, 1994); Maxine Glaz and Jeanne Stevenson Moessner (eds.), *Women in Travail and Transition: A New Pastoral Care* (Minneapolis, Fortress Press, 1991); Marjorie Procter-Smith, *In Her Own Rite: Constructing Feminist Liturgical Tradition* (Nashville, Abingdon Press, 1991); Bonnie J. Miller-McLemore, *Also a Mother: Work and Family as Theological Dilemma* (Nashville, Abingdon Press, 1994).

[7] An effort to grapple with this training is found in Denise M. Ackermann, 'Critical theory, communicative actions and liberating praxis: views of a feminist practical theologian', *Journal of Theology for Southern Africa*, 82 (March 1993), 21-36.

I am perfectly content to be labeled both feminist and practical theologian. In South Africa, however, I prefer to speak of my work as a 'feminist theology of praxis' rather than a 'feminist practical theology' because here the term 'practical theology' is still embedded in a world of which I am not part and whose point of departure is foreign to my enterprise.[8]

In the light of our traumatic history, as evidenced in the painful stories of so many South Africans, the pressing question for a feminist theology of praxis in South Africa is: how can such a theology further the cause of liberation and healing in our society? Herein lies its test for legitimacy. Our theological theories and our praxis are vigilantly scrutinized for their congruence in the ongoing process of action and reflection. I make no apology for focusing on praxis in this article for I believe that it is the task of theology to understand practice, as much as theory, as a source of truth.[9]

Placing healing at the centre

In my context a hermeneutic of healing becomes the core of a feminist theology of praxis. This means that all theological theories and all theological praxis must be measured by their ability to contribute to the healing of my country. What does such a theology have to say to the memories of Nohle Anna Nika-Jonas and Catherine Mlangeni? How do we deal with Joyce Mtimkulu's need to know the truth? What are the implications of Cynthia Ngewu's view of reconciliation for our theological theories and our praxis? Where can Johan find truth?

Healing which is placed at the centre of a feminist theology of praxis, may not be understood as merely an individual quest for

[8] See Ackermann, 'Engaging freedom', pp.37-40.

[9] At the same time a critical stance towards a noetic praxis of theorizing is necessary, see Johann B. Metz, *Faith in History and Society* (New York, Seabury Press, 1980), p. 4. See also Linda Hogan, *From Women's Experience to Feminist Theology* (Sheffield, Sheffield Academic Press, 1995), pp. 64-119 and Patti Lather, *Getting Smart: Feminist Research and Pedagogy with/in the Postmodern* (New York, Routledge, 1991), pp. 11-14, 50-69.

personal healing. Feminists know that the personal and the political cannot be separated. Our crying need is to 'bind up the wounds' at every level and for all in different ways. The cost of apartheid to the humanity of South Africans is incalculable. Spelling out all the dimensions of healing required for a nation, is a task too overwhelming for me to attempt. What is clear is that healing is needed on every level of our lives. Organizing and maintaining the evil of apartheid required compliant interlocking of political, social and religious systems.[10] Penetrating and pervasive healing will take time, even generations, and it requires commitment from and collaboration between politicians, business people, civil society and religious institutions. Social healing is inseparable from political healing because the very politics which shattered so many lives and had such dire effects on the social fabric of South African society, were not only practices of political oppression but were also iniquitous attempts at social engineering. For the process of political and social healing to begin, the victims of apartheid need time to grieve their losses, the opportunity to speak their pain and the right to justice. The perpetrators need healing from racist ideologies, guilt and their lost humanity through acts of acknowledgment, confession and repentance. The present policy of land restitution in which dispossessed people are being returned to their land, is an example of social reparation in the cause of healing. The work of the Trauma Centre for Victims of Violence and Torture in Cape Town founded by Michael Lapsley, himself the victim of a letter bomb, is a further instance of collaboration between psychologists and social scientists and people of faith in the work of healing. My advocacy of communal lament below, is an attempt to contribute to the healing of painful memories of suffering and loss within the community of faith.

In a particularly poignant way, a theology of healing has as key concern the healing of women and children.[11] The fragments

[10] See James N. Poling, *Deliver us from Evil: Resisting Racial and Gender Oppression* (Minneapolis, Fortress Press, 1996), pp. 110-135.

[11] See Jacklyn Cock, *Women and War in South Africa* (Cleveland, The Pilgrim Press, 1993), in particular pp. 213-228.

related at the beginning of this article speak of the pain of mothers and the lost lives of their children, as well as of disillusionment and the search for healing. At a recent hearing of the Truth and Reconciliation Commission in Durban, 'children's voices echoed through the hall, each with a chilling tale about revenge and death'. A committee member describes these stories as the worst ever heard by the Commission 'and we have heard some pretty terrible ones' (*Cape Times,* 15 May 1997). Images from further afield depict women, children and the elderly trudging along dusty roads seeking desperately to escape carnage, standing at open graves and, worst of all, being no more than fly-ridden bodies in camps of death. Sexual violence in which women and children are the victims is endemic at present in South Africa.[12] As a woman I cannot write about healing which does not hold the needs of women and children at its centre.

This search for healing is not only peculiar to my country. It arises from the global nature of crisis. 'To be alive today is to live with pain ... We live in a world come of age, a world no longer innocent about the suffering human beings can inflict on each other,' writes Rita Brock.[13] Wars, sexual violence, the abuse of children in a myriad of ways, the terror camps of North Korea, the killing fields of Bosnia, Burundi, Rwanda and Zaire, famine, poverty and the displacement of people, the systematic rape and plunder of the environment;[14] these and much more are the realities of the late twentieth century. We are a broken world, an age without a name.[15] So the quest for healing praxis is in essence the expression of the dire need for the healing of creation.[16] Human-

[12] Ackermann, ''For such a thing is not done in Israel'', pp. 145-155.

[13] Rita Nakashima Brock, *Journeys by Heart: A Christology of Erotic Power* (New York, Crossroad, 1988), p. 1.

[14] See Denise M. Ackermann and Tahira Joyner, 'Earth-healing in South Africa: challenges to church and mosque' in R. R. Ruether (ed.), *Women Healing Earth: Third World Women on Ecology, Feminism, and Religion* (Maryknoll, Orbis Books, 1996).

[15] David Tracy, 'On naming the present', *Concilium* (1990/1), 66-85.

[16] See Cécé Kolié, 'Jesus as healer?' in R. J. Schreiter (ed.), *Faces of Jesus in Africa* (Maryknoll, Orbis Books, 1991), pp. 128-150.

ity's social, political and spiritual needs are both challenged and encouraged by a theology which places the values of a restored creation at its centre.

Healing praxis, clearly a need for the victims of apartheid, also promises healing for the white community. Years of racist indoctrination within visible, rigid, legislated structures divided our country into 'us' (the powerful, all-knowing, morally superior and God-called minority) and 'them' (the ignorant, heathen masses). Now despair and disillusionment is found among many whites, as illustrated in Johan's cry. This is combined with a shackling fear of the future as a minority 'white tribe'. We too need healing from our self-inflicted wounds of being oppressors as much as we need Cynthia Ngewu's vision of a restored humanity.

For healing praxis to be truly restorative, it has to be collaborative and sustained action for justice, reparation and liberation, based on accountability and empowered by love, hope and passion. It is not the prerogative of any one group of people. It can emerge from the actions and knowledge of those who are suffering, marginalised and oppressed. It can also come from those who have privilege and power, provided they too understand its genesis in the hope for a restored creation and are willing to hear the pain of the suffering of 'the others' and to act in response. Healing praxis is concrete, rooted in the understanding that daily living is not separate from the life of faith. Bread, a roof over one's head, running water and employment are as fundamental to human well-being as are our rights and freedoms.[17] A theology concerned with healing praxis in South Africa seeks economic sustainability and fosters a culture of human rights as a means to finding the wholeness intended by God for a healed world.

The cry for healing is inseparable from the need for justice. In a context whose history is glutted with blatant injustices, doing justice is an inescapable priority. This raises the vexed question of perpetrators who are applying for amnesty to the Truth and Rec-

---

[17] See Mamphela Ramphele, *A Bed Called Home: Life in the Migrant Labour Hostels of Cape Town* (Cape Town, David Philip, 1993) in which the concept of space is elaborated on in the life of migrant dwellers.

onciliation Commission. As their atrocities are revealed, the relatives of victims experience afresh the trauma of loss and grief and, not surprisingly for some, feelings of anger and a desire for retribution. We are learning that justice is more elusive than we had thought and that the need for justice is in this case superseded by the political compromise reached in our negotiated transition to democracy. We remind ourselves constantly that the granting of amnesty was a crucial ingredient in this negotiated settlement, one which prevented the inevitability of a blood bath. Nonetheless, the hunger for justice remains. The moral significance of the victims' anger and the desire for retribution, should not be trivialized or ignored. We may never take for granted, we can only be awed, by Cynthia Ngewu's abandonment of vengeance.[18]

Nature of a feminist theology of praxis

In the light of the need for healing in South Africa, what can a feminist theology of praxis infuse into this process? What is its task and how is its nature shaped by the challenges of our context? A feminist theology of praxis begins by acknowledging the unending, relentless quality of human suffering together with the resilient longing of the human person for wholeness. This double-edged reality insists on a theology which is, in essence, a theology of passion – critical and committed passion. Committed to the cause of healing theories and praxis, it analyses the causes of human suffering. A passion for human well-being is its driving force. But this passion is balanced by critical inquiry and reflection. 'Whatever steps we may take toward ameliorating the misery of existence, we must always recognize that they are practical, provisional, tentative and therefore always demand sustained critical reflection', Marsha Hewitt points out.[19] Passion is not dimmed

---

[18] For an exposition of an ethic of vengeance in the South Africa context, see Willa Boesak, *God's Wrathful Children: Political Oppression and Christian Ethics* (Grand Rapids, W. Eerdmans, 1995).

[19] Marsha A. Hewitt, *Critical Theory of Religion: A Feminist Analysis* (Minneapolis, Fortress Press, 1995), p. 226.

by a critical edge; it is sharpened and tuned into flexible and creative intention. Tempered by a realistic assessment of contextual needs, it is nonetheless driven by a utopian hope for a better world. All good theology, as Beverly Harrison remarks, is utopian, 'in that it envisages a society, a world, a cosmos, in which ...there are 'no excluded ones''.[20]

Second, the material for a feminist theology of praxis emerges from the stories in our different contexts, often stories which have hitherto not been told publically. These stories from the outer circles of discourse, are stories which know the tyranny of the powerful and the refusal to be silenced. The Truth and Reconciliation Commission is creating a forum in which tales of torment and terror are now heard in halls all over our country. The white monolith of chosen ignorance is being cracked. The suffering majority is given a public voice. Memories of suffering are being evoked by the public utterance of private pain. I agree with Donald Shriver that such memories are 'diffused with moral judgment'. As such they are the reverse of the simplistic 'forgive and forget'.[21] That is why they are 'dangerous memories', described by Sharon Welch as 'a people's history of resistance and struggle, of dignity and transcendence in the face of oppression'.[22] These memories are also making known the depths to which those intent on preserving white minority rule were prepared to sink. No theology done in South Africa today can discount these stories.

Whites are also hearing other stories, stories of resistance, of courage and of hope.[23] Testimonies to the resilience of the human

[20] Beverly W. Harrison, *Making the Connections: Essays in Feminist Social Ethics* (Boston, Beacon Press, 1985), p. 236.

[21] Donald Shriver, *An Ethic for Enemies: Forgiveness in Politics* (New York, Oxford University Press, 1995), p. 7.

[22] Sharon D. Welch, *A Feminist Ethic of Risk* (Minneapolis, Fortress Press, 1990), p. 155.

[23] Stories of hope and courage are part of 'struggle' history. See, *inter alia*, Diana E. H. Russell, *Lives of Courage: Women for a New South Africa* (New York, Basic Books, 1991); Cherryl Walker, *Women and Resistance in South Africa* (London, Onyx Press, 1982) and Charles Villa-Vicencio, *The Spirit of Hope: Conversations on Politics, Religion and Values* (Johannesburg, Skotaville, no date).

spirit in which the capacity to survive hell and hope for a new day, also emerge from the grieving hearts of mothers, fathers, relatives, lovers and friends of victims. The silence of the perpetrators is also broken. What emerges is a mixed bag of emotions: relief, anger, fear, remorse, as well as the palpable lack of it. The capacity to truly hear these different stories and to understand their implications, requires an openness of spirit and a willingness to be aware and vulnerable. Once heard and reflected on, these stories will hopefully lead to engaging with a praxis which is healing; transforming old patterns of domination and oppression into better and more humane ways of being.

Third, to seek change actively, requires a collaborative effort between women from different cultures, religious traditions and social locations. No one can effect the kind of healing we require on their own. The task is simply too daunting. Collaborative efforts raise questions of difference and accountability.[24] In a context such as ours, scarred as it is by imposed legislated separatism and by patriarchal structures, we should expect to encounter suspicion and even hostility when differences are either not respected in the rush to find commonalities, or claimed in a separatist way.

Although my work is limited to my experience of my context, I believe that the common human search for healing and wholeness opens opportunities for conversation with women theologians across boundaries of difference. From my perspective this means conversing with women whose views and contexts are different from mine: with African women's theologies, womanist theologies, Asian women's theologies, Mujeristas and Hispanic women and feminist theologians elsewhere. This belief is based on the need for healing in the face of the universality of human

---

[24] See Sneja Gunew and Anna Yeatman (eds.), *Feminism and the Politics of Difference* (Boulder, Westview Press, 1993); Gloria I. Joseph and Jill Lewis, *Common Differences: Conflicts in Black and White Feminist Perspectives* (New York, Anchor Press, 1981); Chandra T. Mohanty, Ann Russo and Lourdes Torres (eds.), *Third World Women and the Politics of Feminism* (Bloomington, Indiana University Press, 1991) and Caroline Ramazanoglu, *Feminism and the Contradictions of Oppression* (London, Routledge, 1989).

suffering. It is also based on a strategic necessity to find common ground for resistance to the manifold oppressions encountered by women.

Fourth, a feminist theology of praxis is embodied practical theology. It accepts that all perceived reality and all knowledge is mediated through our bodies. Our senses are sources of our knowledge. The power to love one another as much as the power to injure another begins in our bodies. We *are* our bodies. The fact that apartheid has done so much damage to the bodies of South Africans, compels us to reflect on the body theologically. Under apartheid our bodies defined our reality with sickening precision. No black bodies in this queue, no black bodies in this bed, no black bodies in this ambulance; no white bodies in shacks, no white bodies in drought stricken 'homelands', no white bodies in broken down class rooms. Our bodies defined whether we were stigmatized or advantaged. Our bodies became the site of the struggle for freedom and a rightful share in our country's resources.

Nancy Eiesland, in her work *The Disabled God,* broadens the feminist understanding of embodiment by setting out a liberatory theology of disability. 'The corporeal is for people with disabilities the most real. Unwilling and unable to take our bodies for granted, we attend to the kinesis of knowledge. That is, we become keenly aware that our physical selves determine our perceptions of the social and physical world'.[25] Later she remarks that the disabled body is the 'center of political struggle'.[26] Her awareness that 'most women with disabilities are impoverished women of color whose homes and bodies have been wracked by war, poverty, and malnutrition' points clearly to the link between the politics of disability and the politics of gender and justice.[27] Eiesland's work opens up new categories of embodiment which are applicable to victims of the struggle in South Africa.

[25] Eiesland, *The Disabled God,* p. 31.
[26] Eiesland, *The Disabled God,* p. 49.
[27] Nancy L. Eiesland, Roundtable on 'Women and disabilities: a challenge to feminist theology', *Journal of Feminist Studies in Religion,* 10:2 (1995), 113-117.

The stories of Nohle Anna Nika-Jonas, Catherine Mlangeni and Joyce Mtimkulu are embodied memories. Hearing these memories into speech, to paraphrase Nelle Morton's striking phrase,[28] evokes bodily pain. Speakers become witnesses for loved ones who are no longer. More than being witnesses, they become agents for change as history is re-written. These uncovered memories of injustices and injuries are also tough moral judgements which make a powerful call for justice to be done. The work of justice and healing is 'body work' just as much as the struggle for liberation called for committed bodies.

Fifth, despite postmodern predictions of the demise of imagination, the nature of a feminist theology of praxis is essentially imaginative.[29] When it dares to dream its utopian dreams for a better world and when hopes are translated into actions for healing and wholeness, imagination remains a vital ingredient. Daring and imaginative praxis was at the heart of the struggle for liberation in South Africa: defiance campaigns, marches, innovative methods of protest. The kind of imaginative praxis which is effective and constructive is one which calls for the creative convergence of the poetic and the ethical.[30]

To be ethically imaginative is to be prepared to stand alongside 'the others', the suffering and the marginalised, to hear the cry of need and then, compelled by the ethical demands of imagination, to respond to need with healing praxis. Acts of imagination are ethically accountable to the common desire for justice and healing and as such are tested in community. The work of the Truth and Reconciliation Commission is, in itself, daring imaginative praxis for accountability and truth.

[28] Nelle Morton, *The Journey is Home* (Boston, Beacon Press, 1985), pp. 127-128.
[29] See Richard Kearney, *The Wake of Imagination: Toward a Postmodern Culture* (Minneapolis, University of Minnesota Press, 1988), pp. 359-361. See also Denise M. Ackermann ''The substance of things hoped for': imaginative praxis' in forthcoming Festschrift for Riet Bons-Storm, edited by Maaike de Haardt, Els Maeckelberghe and Mathilde van Dijk, (Kampen, Kok/Pharos) which draws on the imaginative actions of the Black Sash, a women's human rights organisation, during the apartheid struggle.
[30] Kearney, *The Wake of Imagination*, pp. 361-371.

Resistance to apartheid seized on the poetic nature of imaginative praxis by using art, drama, literature, poetry, street art, innovative posters and other means to express itself.[31] Christianity itself is richly endowed with the poetic expression of the imagination through its use of symbols, rites, stories and metaphors. The poetic does not exist in some abstract realm. The essence of what is perceived as real finds expression through poetic images because they are, in themselves, experiences of what is real. The work of healing draws on the human ability to imagine and hope for wholeness.

Sixth, the concern with healing is undergirded by the belief in the role of human agency in the mending of God's creation. In Elaine Scarry's words: 'Belief is the act of imagining'.[32] The Christian hope for the actualizing of the 'reign of God', when love, justice, freedom, peace and wholeness will flourish, provides the moral imperative for healing actions. We have to struggle to hold on to this utopian vision while we act as agents for bringing it about. Our hopes are not only eschatologically garbed but rest firmly in the desire for historical transformation. 'This [hope] in Cornel West's term, is a utopian realism: an anticipation of a new, transfigured reality based on a realistic analysis of the sufferings and desires of the present age'.[33] Living one's hope for a better world means realistically acknowledging brokenness and need while at the same time engaging with life in such a way that deeds express that which one hopes for. Human agency and hope combine in the search for healing. We have to make our hopes happen.

Finally, a feminist theology of praxis is characterized by risk and requires stamina. Ambitious and risky, it is an exercise in vulnerability. It risks failing, it risks appearing futile in the face of

---

[31] Gavin Younge, *Art of the South African Townships* (New York, Rizzoli, 1988).

[32] Elaine Scarry, *The Body in Pain: The Making and Unmaking of the World* (New York, Oxford University Press, 1985), p.205.

[33] From Rebecca S. Chopp and Mark L. Taylor, *Reconstructing Christian Theology* (Minneapolis, Fortress Press, 1994), p. 2, quotation from Cornel West, *The American Evasion of Philosophy: a Genealogy of Pragmatism* (Madison, University of Wisconsin Press, 1989).

often overwhelming odds. The voices in Ramah will continue to cry out (Jer 31:15, Mt 2:18). For those who choose not to be deaf, the cries of human suffering everywhere call us to seek healing, even when we have no illusions about the enormity of the task.

Healing praxis: awareness, accountability and forgiveness

'The beginning of the path of healing is the end of life unlived'.[34] I understand the 'life unlived' as a life barren of self-reflection, which is narcissistic and disconnected from people, particularly from those who are 'different'. Healing praxis starts with awareness, or what the Buddhist monk, Thich Nhat Hahn, calls 'mindfulness'.[35] Awareness is the willingness to hear, to see and to feel. Once stories, like those presently being told, are truly heard, the 'unlived life' ends and the slow painful process of transformation begins. Johan's painful cry is an example of such an awakening. The longing for changes that will mend the world, is born in awareness. For most white South Africans, mindfulness or awareness is a waking up, a willingness to forego the sleep of chosen ignorance and to face the grim and exacting reality of our history and the legacies of apartheid. As Adrienne Rich perceptively suggests, questions of historical responsibility, questions of historical consciousness and ignorance need to be examined in terms of power.[36] Unbridled power thrives on lack of awareness and the unwillingness to accept historical responsibility.

To those who plead ignorance, who say 'But I did not know', the answer, in Rich's words, is: '[We] are born both innocent and accountable'.[37] We are innocent in the sense that we do not choose

---

[34] Stephen Levine, *Healing into Life and Death* (Bath, Gateway Books, 1987), p. 88.

[35] Thich Nhat Hanh, *The Miracle of Mindfulness: a Manual on Meditation*, tr. Mobi Ho (Boston, Beacon Press, 1974).

[36] Adrienne Rich, 'Resisting Amnesia' in *Blood, Bread and Poetry: Selected Prose 1979-1985* (New York, W. W. Norton, 1986), p. 137.

[37] Rich, *Blood, Bread and Poetry*, pp. 144-145.

the place, time and condition into which we are born. We all carry within ourselves the behaviour patterns and assumptions of the group we belong to. We are accountable because we have moral agency. I can choose to become either consciously historical or to be 'a technician of amnesia and nostalgia, one who dulls the imagination by starving it or feeding it with junk food'.[38] Despite the fact that apartheid as a system was successful in separating people, despite the fact that white South Africans were subjected to a great deal of ideological indoctrination, if we did not know it was because we chose not to know. Yes, we are born innocent and we become accountable.

Acceptance of accountability is the next step in the healing process. Elsewhere I have written that our relationships are by nature reciprocal and that '[r]eciprocity calls for accountability. We are bound in relationships that claim responses, that make us accountable and, in our very accountability, bonds of relationship are forged, strengthened and expanded'.[39] We all have our communities of accountability. These communities shape our identities and our theologies through transmission of traditions, cultural norms, social mores, customs, ritual and myth. The healing we require is one which combines both a rigorous accountability to our different communities and histories with a reaching out across differences to 'the other', seeking collaboration in the cause of healing, and being prepared to be vulnerable yet actively contributing and concerned citizens.

The work of the Truth and Reconciliation Commission is an exercise in accountability. Victims recount, perpetrators are called to account. Processes of truth-telling and justice-seeking in which abusers of human rights are called to account, should ideally become part of the fabric of our society, so that all who hold power, both in the present and in the future, are held accountable for their actions at all times. We need the courage and insight to face *all* manifestations of lack of accountability in order for healing to continue.

---

[38] Rich, *Blood, Bread and Poetry*, p. 145.
[39] Ackermann, 'Engaging freedom', p. 45.

The temptation for Christians is to move from confession to forgiveness with unseemly haste under the guise of complying with Christian values. This is both a misunderstanding of the nature of Christian forgiveness and a move which will not effect reconciliation, but rather lead to the repression of bitterness and hatred.

Christians are aware that forgiveness is central to our faith. Too often, however, it is seen primarily as absolution from private guilt. This is a limited, even cheap view of forgiveness. Forgiveness is not a private affair. Neither is forgiveness in South Africa a purely political matter. While I agree with Shriver in his compelling study, *An Ethic for Enemies,* that the idea of forgiveness has too often suffered from religious captivity, I cannot speak only of political forgiveness.[40] The kind of forgiveness required in the South African context is one which does not separate forgiveness into political versus private forgiveness. Forgiveness is a way of life lived in fidelity to our hopes and our responsibilities for a restored creation. Cheap forgiveness is like cheap grace. As Dietrich Bonhoeffer warned: 'Cheap grace is the preaching of forgiveness without requiring repentance'.[41] For Bonhoeffer, true repentance is embodied in a life of discipleship. Forgiveness is thus costly. Forgiveness cannot be demanded. It can only be hoped for. The aim of forgiveness is to restore communion with one another and with God in order to reconcile our brokenness. Forgiveness is a way of life.

The tales of terror and torment, the anger and the grief of those testifying before the Truth and Reconciliation Commission, are moments of recovered memories of wrongs, injustices and injuries. They are also powerful moral judgments. Shriver points out that

> Forgiveness, in politics or in any other human relation, does not require the abandonment of all versions of punishment of evildoers. But it does require the abandonment of *vengeance*, and this is its second constituent. Forgiveness gets its real start under the double impetus of judgment and forbearance from revenge. Forbear-

---

[40] Shriver, *An Ethic for Enemies*, p. 7.

[41] Dietrich Bonhoeffer, *The Cost of Discipleship*, 13th imp (London, SCM Press, 1984), p. 36.

ance opens the door toward a future that will not repeat the old crimes. Unaccompanied by forbearance in this very beginning, moral judgment often fuels new enmity.[42]

Nietzsche was right. Christian teachings about love and forgiveness have not acknowledged people's desires for revenge; they have rather masked and repressed them.[43] Healing processes can only begin by acknowledging the trauma of victims in its entirety, including their feelings of moral outrage and their desires for retribution. The moral judgment and the forbearance from vengeance are the prerogative of the victims.

In this process, reconciliation cannot be spoken of except possibly as a word to describe what *may* happen at the end of such a process. Forgiveness takes time and it is not to be hurried. Anger and pain are expressed, over and over again, articulated and experienced in a process in which the causes of suffering are probed, questioned and railed against by each victim according to her or his needs. Forgiveness is also linked to the need for justice, repentance and reparation. Repentance signifies accountability, a change of behaviour and an understanding of restitution. Once perpetrators repent, there must be the willingness to wait and to hope for the renewal of human relationship with quiet forbearance, accepting that one is never in the position of calling for forgiveness. When forgiveness meets repentance, reconciliation becomes possible.

Communities of faith: healing praxis in lament and the eucharist

My faith has largely been nurtured in small communities outside the church. The church has too often been an uncomfortable, ambiguous place where my search for affirmation and belonging has encountered many of the barriers familiar to feminist women.

---

[42] Shriver, *An Ethic for Enemies*, p. 7.
[43] Friedrich Nietzsche, *On the Genealogy of Morals*, tr. W. Kaufmann and R. J. Hollingdale, ed. W. Kaufmann (New York, Vintage Books, 1989), essay 1, section 14.

This experience has led me to differentiate between the institutional church and communities of faith. Communities of faith include those people, many of whom are women, who profess faith but who, for a number of reasons, find themselves outside the church. Such communities also include small groups of people who, although they are members of the church, cannot ignore the tug of their hearts to share and explore faith together in environments which favour closeness.

Despite the obstacles of male-dominance, exclusive language and discriminating practices, I still belong to my church and I continue to write hoping to be heard in the church.[44] Why? Chiefly for two reasons. First, in the communal sharing of the bread and the wine I have found grace and food for life. I am at heart a eucharistic being. Second, the church, despite its ambivalent role in combating racism, afforded me a place to join other critical voices in opposing apartheid. Now, my feelings of disquiet about the ethical and moral basis of our emerging society have made one thing clear: I want to continue the pursuit of justice, healing and freedom for my society as a member of my church. This ongoing struggle needs the nurturing of the bread and the wine, shared in community.

This ambiguous experience of finding sustenance both in small groups and in the rites of the eucharist merge in a feminist theological search for healing praxis. I have little faith in the ability of the institutional church to transform itself, certainly not speedily enough to be able to deal with the present pain of people. I do believe in the efficacy of small groups within the church. In the present climate of truth-telling, small groups have much to offer people who are willing to share their stories. A commitment to hear 'the other' and to respect the validity of her or his story in a common search for healing, is the ground rule for such groups. As stories unfold, awareness increases. We do not only hear the sto-

---

[44] See Denise M. Ackermann, Jonathan Draper and Emma Mashinini (eds.), *Women Hold Up Half the Sky: Women in the Church in Southern Africa* (Pietermaritzburg, Cluster Publications, 1991).

ries of others. We have our own stories to tell. As these stories intersect, they change and we too are changed. Not all stories are liberating or comforting; stories can reinforce oppressions. But when these stories and the truths of our faith enter into conversation with one another, our longings for healing and wholeness and our faith in God's promises of a mended world, touch our consciousness in new ways. Momentarily we glimpse our restored humanity.

Engaging with stories alone, is not enough. The most important aspect of this shared search for healing lies in embracing communal lament. We have so much to lament about.[45] Traditionally, lament has been the prerogative of the suffering victims. The psalms of communal lament,[46] the stories of Rachel, Hagar, Hannah, David and Job, express the cries of suffering people, seeking deliverance from God. Nohle Anna Nika-Jonas, Catherine Mlangeni, Cynthia Ngewu and Joyce Mtimkulu together with thousands of others who share their grief, have decades of suffering and loss to lament. It is their prerogative.

The question arises: is lament appropriate for whites in South Africa? Can we like David, lament, from 'the other side'? Can we afford not to lament? We need to cry out to God for deliverance from our shameful past and for healing from the wounds that perpetrators inflict on themselves as well as on others. The particular suffering born out of the growing awareness of our role in the history of our country, should be lamented. We can lament the misuse of power and privilege, and our lack of courage in not standing up to evil and injustice. Mothers can lament for their sons drafted into the defence force and emerging after two years, scarred and depressed, cynical or ready to leave for far shores while at the same time remembering other mothers whose sons were tortured, imprisoned, killed and exiled in cause of the same ideology of white power.

---

[45] Denise M. Ackermann, 'On hearing and lamenting: faith and truth-telling' in Botman and Petersen (eds.), *To Remember and to Heal*, pp. 47-56.

[46] For examples, see Ps. 44, 60, 74, 79, 80, 83 and 89.

Lament is never utilitarian. It is an existential wail which comes from the human soul. The hope is that communal lament of people in small groups in which the lamentation of the afflicted is heard and responded to, will make for healing and the restoration of well-being. Although lament is expressed communally, it comes from individual hearts which are weeping and raging, seeking a response from God. The very nature of lament is profoundly spiritual and profoundly political. Remorse, anger, the need for accountability and justice, combine as we contend with God.

Sadly, Western Christianity has lost its ability to lament. Acts of lamentation have disappeared from our liturgies in our churches. Keening bodies addressing God directly, calling God to account for the intractability of suffering, are deemed to be liturgically inappropriate in mainline Christianity in my country. Yet, at the same time, at African funerals in townships and rural areas, women lead the communal lament which often lasts for days. These cultural and religious rituals of lament are, however, abandoned at the church door. Is their repudiation attributable to the fact that women lead the lament? Is the very bodiliness of lament too menacing to those who want to maintain authority through tight control of liturgical actions? Does the fact that the people take initiative and address God without intermediaries threaten the role of the clergy? The loss of lament is costly, not least of all because it is crucial in the search for healing.[47]

Facing the irresoluble enigma of human suffering and then learning to live in that vacillating zone between acceptance and rebellion, is strangely healing. The psalms have much to teach us here. Lament of victims dares to rail against God and the inexplicability of suffering. Then, virtually in the same breath, it turns to praise. Divine silence is assaulted with tears, petitions and then with praise. In the midst of all the questioning, we find a God in whom we can truly trust. In Walter Brueggemann's words, we find a God 'whose impotence is reshaped by pathos'.[48] Lament of

---

[47] See Walter Brueggemann, 'The costly loss of lament', in his work *The Psalms and the Life of Faith* (Minneapolis, Fortress Press, 1994), pp. 98-111.

[48] Brueggemann, *The Psalms*, p. 108.

perpetrators emerges from anguished guilt, heartfelt repentance and the desperate search for the grace of forgiveness and acceptance. The outcome of this search is affirmed by the fact that such lament also ends on a note of praise and hope. Lament is to move from 'candor about suffering [to] gratitude about hope'.[49]

Lamenting alone is not enough. Having keened and raged, wept and repented, we then recognise two further needs: the first is to wait in faith; the second is to place the tears and the acts of love in the communion cup. God, we are told, is good to those who seek and wait; 'It is good that one should wait patiently for the salvation of the Lord' (Lam 3:26). Waiting is an act of faith which requires risk and holds on to hope. Perhaps, in the waiting, the institutional church will see and hear the lament of these small groups of people. And then, who knows, lament may be recovered for the worshipping community.

In the waiting, we seek food for new life in the bread and the wine. These are testing moments, filled with doubts and stumbling blocks. Can we in the face of so much human suffering, remember God's justice, mercy and love at the table? Do we trust that God's work of making all things new, as revealed in the life and work of Jesus Christ, is ongoing and affirmed by our remembrance of what happened in the upper room? A further stumbling block is the continuing dominance of the eucharist by the largely male clergy. This has not only protected male power in the church but it has also separated the clergy from the laity, rendering the laity largely passive.[50] If the eucharist is a powerful symbol of sexism and separation, can it be a potentially healing rite?

When racist laws kept people apart in my country, the eucharistic rite of sharing one cup took on revolutionary significance. At some altar rails there was no apartheid. Further exploration of the radical implications of the eucharist calls for imaginative praxis. By combining memory and imagination, a feminist theology of

[49] Brueggemann, *The Psalms*, p. 196.
[50] See Rosemary Radford Ruether, *Women-Church: Theology and Practice of Feminist Liturgical Communities* (San Francisco, Harper and Row, 1985), pp. 75-95 for the implications of clericalism.

praxis seeks to expand the meaning of the eucharist so that its
potential for remembering, healing and transforming is realised
more fully. 'The eucharist should be the symbol of our nurture,
growth, and participation in the authentic human life of mutual
empowerment', writes Rosemary Ruether.[51] For the small groups
who, in trust, have lamented and praised together, the need to take
these initial healing processes into the ritual of breaking bread and
sharing the cup, is further affirmation that the life, ministry and
death of Jesus offers us new life. This affirmation we express in
ritual.

All human beings have a longing for ritual. All 'human life is
shot through and through with ritual', writes Susanne Langer. She
continues 'It is an intricate fabric of reason and rite, of knowledge
and religion, prose and poetry, fact and dream'.[52] Human creativity, longing, need and faith come together when groups seek ways
of expressing new found relationships. The eucharist holds this
promise.

'Rituals are about relationships; religious rituals are about ultimate relationships – about a people's origins and destiny and their
true identity and purpose even in ordinary life', writes Mary
Collins. Healed relationships are our compelling need. She continues: 'People learn who they are and who they are becoming before
God in their very physical positions and their assigned roles in
sacred assemblies, by what they themselves do and say, by what is
said and done to them and for them, by the transaction in which
their participation is either prescribed or proscribed'.[53] When ritual
learning it taken away from the people by clerical dominance of
the sacraments, healing is delayed or impeded. Shared lament
needs to be cemented promptly in the cup as a further affirmation
that the healing is happening.

[51] Ruether, *Women-Church*, p. 77.
[52] Susanne K. Langer, *Philosophy in a New Key: A Study in the Symbolism of
Reason, Rite, and Art,* 3rd edn (Cambridge, Mass., Harvard University Press,
1979), p. 36.
[53] Mary Collins, *Worship: Renewal to Practice* (Washington, The Pastoral
Press, 1987), p. 259.

I imagine small, vital groups of people who, after lamenting together, give thanks for memories of God's loving power in the past and thereby affirm this power in the present. And, most importantly, faith in God's present desire to love, equips us to resist future evil. In particular God's dealings with women, children, the poor and the vulnerable, are remembered through recalling shared stories. This combination of memory and thanksgiving forges a new solidarity which is focused on Jesus, the one who was anointed to bring good news to the poor, to proclaim release to the captives, recovery of sight to the blind and freedom for the captives.

Images of the very earliest celebrations of the eucharist feed my imagination: small groups of people meeting to break bread and drink wine, singing, praying and remembering the gospel events.[54] I imagine a eucharist which is celebrated in small groups seeking reconciliation across historical chasms caused by apartheid and across the divides of patriarchal ideologies. Eucharist, in essence thanksgiving, expresses our gratitude, our reasons for blessing God. How fitting to move from lament, to praise and then to be able to give thanks.[55] Those who have benefitted from being on the side of the oppressors need to examine what sacrifices they are called on to make which will advance healing of fractured relationships. Men are called to re-examine their places of power and participation in sexist systems. Victims are faced with grappling with the ideas of forgiveness and reconciliation as members of the community of faith.

These are complicated processes. For white women, for instance, the need to sacrifice unjust privileges which the apartheid years showered on us, is clear. Equally clear is the fact that we have experienced sexism and its demands for sacrifice. Oppressing and being oppressed are not neatly separated in our lives. The very idea

[54] See Gregory Dix, *The Shape of the Liturgy*, 2nd edn (London, Adam and Charles Black, 1978), pp. 16-21 and Robert Cabié, *The Church at Prayer: An Introduction to the Liturgy* (ed. A. G. Martimort), vol. 2: *The Eucharist* (London, Cassell Ltd., 1986), pp. 36-38, 239-240.

[55] Cabié, *The Church at Prayer*, pp. 21, 26-29, 93-94.

of sacrifice requires in Marjorie Procter-Smith's words 'a high degree of discernment and the knowledge of intersecting oppressions ...

Therefore an emancipatory use of the eucharistic motif of sacrifice must be informed by critical consciousness about both the demand for sacrifice of unjust power and the complexity of interlocking oppressions'.[56]

The community of faith, gathered to eat the bread and drink the wine, image the body of Christ in the suffering world. We recollect the suffering and the death of women, children and the victims of apartheid, as we recollect Christ's suffering and death. 'A voice is heard in Ramah, lamentation and bitter weeping...'. In the cup, suffering and memory fuse into the transforming power of God's love. We move from despair and brokenness into hope and healing. 'The Eucharist as eschatological feast offers imaginative hope, the visionary experience of the goal toward which we work in our daily struggle'.[57] As we celebrate we pray

> God bless Africa.
> Guard her children.
> Guide her rulers,
> And give her peace for Jesus Christ's sake, Amen.[58]

A final fragment

In May 1993, I visited Mozambique at the invitation of Bishop Dinis Sengulane, the Anglican Bishop of Lebombo. Together with Francis Cull, the seventy-eight year old director of the Institute for Christian Spirituality, we held workshops for the church in small communities who were trying to come together again after being uprooted during the long years of civil war. On our last evening in

---

[56] Procter-Smith, *In Her Own Rite,* p.162.

[57] Procter-Smith, *In Her Own Rite*, p. 163.

[58] This prayer the Anglican church in South Africa owes to Trevor Huddleston, a monk of the Community of the Resurrection, who allied himself to black resistance to apartheid in the 1950s.

Maputo I was resting after a long and tiring drive from the north when the Bishop insisted that we accompany him to his chapel.

I shall never forget what followed. Fourteen year old Candida stood before the baptismal font. Her parents watched her anxiously. Two years previously, during preparation for confirmation and baptism, she had been abducted by Renamo forces when on a visit to her relatives outside Maputo,. She had reappeared out of the bush that morning, her adolescent body criss-crossed by strips of rags 'to ward off evil'. Her father contacted the Bishop and said: 'She was ready two years ago. I am bringing her to church tonight. You must baptise and confirm her right away.' Watching Candida in her broken plastic sandals and old pink spotted dress, I saw trauma, disorientation and fear. I could hardly bear to think of what she had been through. My mind raced through a list of remedies – medication for trauma, long term therapy, tests for HIV. But in May 1993, Mozambique had no psychiatrists, psychotherapists or pathologists. Her parents did what they could. They brought her for initiation into the community of faith, to be covered with the prayers of the church and fed with the bread and the wine – the sole means of grace and healing available to the people of Maputo.

ADDITIONAL BIBLIOGRAPHY

Benhabib, S., Butler, J., Cornell, D. and Fraser, N. *Feminist Contentions: A Philosophical Exchange*, New York, Routledge, 1995

Habermas, J. *Theory and Practice*, tr. J. Viertel, Boston, Beacon Press, 1973

Hampson, D. (ed.). *Swallowing a Fishbone: Feminist Theologians Debate Christianity*, London, SPCK, 1996

Huber, W. *Violence: The Unrelenting Assault on Human Dignity*, tr. R.C. L. Gritsch, Minneapolis, Fortress Press, 1996

Kappeler, S. *The Will to Violence: The Politics of Personal Behaviour*, New York, Teachers College Press, Columbia University, 1995

King, U. (ed.). *Feminist Theology from the Third World: A Reader*, London, SPCK, 1994

Mananzan, M. J., Oduyoye, M. A., Tamez, E., Clarkson, J. S., Grey, M. C. and Russell, L. M. (eds.). *Women Resisting Violence: Spirituality for Life*, Maryknoll, Orbis Books, 1996

Meehan, Johanna (ed.). *Feminists Read Habermas: Gendering the Subject of Discourse,* New York, Routledge, 1995

Norris, K. *The Cloister Walk,* New York, Riverhead Books, 1996

Oduyoye, M. A. *Daughters of Anowa: African Women and Patriarchy,* Maryknoll, Orbis Books, 1995

Oduyoye, M. A. and Kanyoro, M. R. A. (eds.). *The Will to Arise: Women, Tradition, and the Church in Africa,* Maryknoll, Orbis Books, 1993

Procter-Smith, M. and Walton, J. R. (eds.). *Women at Worship: Interpretations of North American Diversity,* Louisville, Westminster/John Knox Press, 1993

Sands, K. M. *Escape from Paradise: Evil and Tragedy in Feminist Theology,* Minneapolis, Fortress Press, 1994

Schreiter, R. J. *Constructing Local Theologies,* Maryknoll, Orbis Books, 1985

Schreiter, R. J. *Reconciliation: Mission and Ministry in a Changing Social Order,* Maryknoll, Orbis Books, 1992

Sölle, D. *Suffering,* tr. E. R. Kalin, Philadelphia, Fortress Press, 1975

Tutu, D. *An African Prayer Book,* New York, Doubleday, 1995

Ward, H., Wild, J. and Morley, J. (eds.). *Celebrating Women,* London, SPCK, 1995

VI

Things not seen:
women with physical disabilities,
oppression and practical theology

Nancy L. EIESLAND[1]

As a woman with disabilities, a sociologist of religion, and a professor at a seminary in the United States, I view practical theology as a scholarly resource for forming and communicating the sociological endeavor within a theological context. That is, I view some approaches to practical theology as bridges between, on the one hand, the social sciences that see their primary tasks as description, interpretation, and sometimes explanation, and, on the other, theology that understands its crucial tasks as moral suasion, normative judgment, and religious reflection. Practical theology can be a vehicle for pragmatic, socially informed moral and theological analysis. This type of practical theology shares such emphases from the sociological tradition of critical theory as sensitivity to power and power relations in all social situations; recognition of the situated character of the production of all knowledge; and advocacy for improvement in people's lives. Practical theology that underscores the particularity of our circumstances can also reveal the situated character of our struggles with God and as God's people.

In my earlier work, I have highlighted the importance of an accessible practical theological method in the creation of a liberatory the-

[1] I am very grateful to Dinah Shelly whose helpful suggestions substantially improved this paper. Many thanks to the editors of this volume for their insightful directions.

ology of disability.[2] This approach follows the lead of Rebecca S. Chopp who argues for a critical praxis correlation method that recognizes the fundamental multiplicity of human experiences as the basis for theological reflection and that underscores the history of oppression and exclusion within the church as well as in societies at large.[3] A liberatory theology of disability that engages difference, specificity, and embodiment and that brings into being solidarity, anticipation and transformation begins, I argue, with the lament. The lament is both a descriptive and theological act.

In her book *Suffering*, Dorothee Sölle reminds us that intense suffering and oppression often deprives its victims of the ability to speak about their experience.[4] These deprivations take many forms. The suffering person may lack language that places the suffering in its social context, instead viewing it as a personal fault or as essential to the ordering of the universe. Such views on suffering render it unspeakable. That is, misery must be hidden or accepted, rather than named publicly and transformed. Yet when suffering is voiced and shared, it can create solidarity between people who suffer similarly.

Sölle develops this point by distinguishing three phases in the suffering process. To move from the first phase of silence, which is characterized by isolation and powerlessness, to the third phase of creating change which is distinguished by solidarity with others, she argues that it is necessary to move through the second stage of lamenting, characterized by the expression and communication of one's pain and placing that pain in its social context. Moving from silence to speech for the oppressed is a gesture of defiance that heals, that makes new life and growth possible. The sufferer who cannot speak about her suffering at best will be shut off from new life, at worst be destroyed by that explosive rage or

---

[2] N. Eiesland, *The Disabled God: Toward a Liberatory Theology of Disability* (Nashville, Abingdon, 1994).

[3] R. S. Chopp, 'Practical Theology and Liberation' in L. S. Mudge and J. N. Poling (eds.), *Formation and Reflection* (Philadelphia, Fortress, 1987), pp. 130-141.

[4] D. Sölle, *Suffering*, translated by E.R. Kalin (Philadelphia, Fortress Press, 1975).

insipid despair that drives the sufferer to consider actions she would not ordinarily take. The silence must be broken; we must raise the lament in order that change can be actualized.

This essay is a lament against the oppression that too many women with disabilities experience daily. Raising the protest and learning to lament is no easy feat for anyone, but perhaps especially for women with disabilities. As a woman with a congenital disability, I grew up learning that complaining was a nasty habit that I should not acquire. As a young girl, I learned that the agonies of physical pain and familial and social abuse were not to be spoken aloud. The only route to social acceptability for a girl with a disability was to be amiable, smile, and never complain. Having learned my lesson well, I was selected as a poster child for the March of Dimes. I was so sweet; I never complained.

But there was much to protest; and it would be years before I was able to raise the true complaints of a former poster child. In writing *The Disabled God*, I began to lament the situation of too many Christians with disabilities who were practically excluded from the covenants of our own tradition. In writing that work, I learned the theological place of the lament. Here I will focus my lamentations on the specific experiences of many women with disabilities in North America. I begin the protest with a careful analysis of the social context of women with disabilities in the United States. I address the development of the disability rights movement and women's difficulties within it. Next, I frame the discussion of women's oppression in dominant society using Iris Marion Young's multi-faceted explication of oppression. Young describes the 'faces' of oppression as involving marginalization, exploitation, powerlessness, cultural imperialism, violence. In discussing each face, I define Young's terms as I address it in the case of people with disabilities and, in particular, women with physical disabilities.[5] Young's social theory enables us to move beyond a

---

[5] I. M. Young, *Justice and the Politics of Difference* (Princeton, Princeton University Press, 1990), pp. 48-63. For additional discussion of men with disabilities, see T. J. Gerschick and A. S. Miller, 'Gender Identities at the Crossroads of Masculinity and Physical Disability', *Masculinities*, 2:1 (1995), 34-55.

description of the oppression of women with disabilities to an interpretation of their experience in terms of the wider society. Finally, I turn to practical theology in order to bridge the questions of religious belief and practice.

Framing oppression of women with disabilities

Beginning in the mid-1960s in the United States, a collective, grass-roots protest against oppression of people with disabilities was arising. Identifying barriers to full inclusion, speaking about cultural bias based on beliefs about people with disabilities, and organizing for self-empowerment was the three-fold aim of the nascent disability rights movement. In contrast to the rehabilitation models of disability, disability rights activists advanced a sociopolitical perspective that highlighted legislative redress of discrimination and fostered an emphasis on independent living and self-advocacy. In the United States, the disability rights movement emerged from the independent living movement that resulted in the establishment of the first Centers for Independent Living (CIL) in California and other cities across the nation in the 1960s. Circumventing the near total control over essential services wielded by governmental agencies and medical institutions, these CILs acted as clearinghouses for information on housing, transportation, education and facilitated direct contact with attendants and other service providers. Control of vital resources enabled many people with disabilities to control the terms of their self-definition, as well.

As the movement expanded, it began to define people with disabilities as a minority group whose minority status results initially not from any shared physical or cultural characteristics but rather from being singled out by others in the society in which they live for differential and unequal treatment.[6] Since the 1970s, an expan-

---

[6] For an overview of the history of the disability rights movement, see J. Shapiro, *No Pity: People with Disabilities Forging a New Civil Rights Movement* (New York, Times Books, 1994).

sive community of and literature by people with disabilities has
emerged, writing their own history, creating their own images in
literature and art, and developing their own theories of disability.
Thus the minority group of people with disabilities is now not only
perceived as a function of social exclusion, but also as a result of
the construction of a distinct subcultural perspective.[7] Perceiving
people with disabilities as members of a minority group, rather
than as victims of a private physical, mental or emotional tragedy,
or as unemployable or medically dependent individuals, has provided the framework for understanding how oppression functions
in the lives of people with disabilities. It has enabled them to make
public their too often private oppressions.

Nonetheless, despite the disability rights movement's identification of *all* people with disabilities as part of a distinct and fluid
minority group, women with disabilities in the movement have
often found their concerns dismissed as private matters, not worthy
of public lobbying efforts or civic discussion. Furthermore, the
mobilized constituency of the disability rights movement has generally represented the concerns of white, middle-class people with
disabilities. This perspective, while important, neglects many
women (and men) with disabilities who are impoverished people of
color and those whose bodies have been wracked by abuse,
poverty, and malnutrition. Women with disabilities have developed
feminist analyses of their experience inside and outside the disability rights movement to link their experiences of gender, race, ethnicity, and sexual orientation to their experiences of disability.[8] The

---

[7] S. R. Whyte and B. Ingstad, 'Disability and Culture: An Overview' in B.
Ingstad and S. R. Whyte (eds.), *Disability and Culture* (Berkeley, University of
California Press, 1995), pp. 3-32; J. Callahan, *Don't Worry. He Won't get Far on
Foot* (New York, Random House, 1989).

[8] It is beyond the scope of this essay fully to address the emergence of feminist
disability studies. For careful attention to the development of these perspectives,
see N. Eiesland, 'Religion and Disability Studies: Thoughts on the Status and
Future of an Emerging Dialogue', *Disability Studies Quarterly*, 15:3 (1995), 4-9;
Roundtable on 'Women with Disabilities: A Challenge to Feminist Theology',
Journal of Feminist Studies in Religion, 10:2 (1995), 113-116; B. Hillyer, *Feminism and Disability* (Norman, University of Oklahoma Press, 1993); and, S. Wen-
dell, 'Toward a Feminist Theory of Disability', *Hypatia*, 4:2 (1993), 104-124.

achievements of the disability rights movement and women's voices within it have related to their enhanced ability to name the circumstances of their lives.

In describing the social situation of women with disabilities, I use the dual frames of Iris Marion Young's analysis of justice from the lived experience of its absence among dominated and oppressed people and of disability studies taken generally as an emergent discipline. In *Justice and the Politics of Difference*, Young employs modern and postmodern philosophical, sociological, and psychological theories to reveal how conceptions of knowledge legitimate daily lived practices of oppression and to make substantive proposals for change arising out of the experience of oppressed social groups. Locating herself in the experience of insurgent social groups, Young writes, 'rational reflection on justice begins in hearing, in heeding a call rather than in asserting and mastering a state of affairs, however ideal'.[9] Justice begins with the relationship of speaking and listening.

Young identifies justice as relating primarily to politics which, in turn, concerns all aspects of institutional organization, public activity, social practices and habits, and content. Justice itself is the 'virtue of citizenship, of persons deliberating about problems and issues that confront them collectively in our institutions and actions, under conditions without domination or oppression, with reciprocity and mutual tolerance of difference'.[10] She also explicitly expands the notion of citizenship toward a conception of a heterogeneous public in which individual and group differences are recognized and respected, though not entirely understood.

Finally, Young develops a group-focused delineation of the faces of oppression that will be discussed more extensively below. Oppression is a structural phenomenon although it is frequently enacted interpersonally. The common character of oppression experienced by a social group is the 'inhibition of their ability to

[9] Young, *Justice and the Politics of Difference*, p.5.
[10] Young, *Justice and the Politics of Difference*, pp.33-34.

develop and exercise their capacities and express their needs, thoughts, and feelings'.[11] The 'faces' that oppression presents include: marginalization, exploitation, powerlessness, cultural imperialism and violence.

The second frame used in describing the situation of women with disabilities is the emerging academic field of disability studies, which emanates from and supports the disability rights movement. Largely located within the disciplines of sociology and medical anthropology, disability studies reframes the consideration of disability by focusing on it as a social phenomenon, social construct, metaphor, and culture, utilizing a minority group model. It examines ideas related to disability in all forms of cultural representation throughout history, and examines the policies and practices of all societies, to understand the social, rather than the physical or psychological determinants of the experience of disability. This focus shifts the emphasis from a prevention/treatment/remediation paradigm, to a social/cultural/ political paradigm. Disability studies has been developed to disentangle impairments from the myth, ideology, and stigma that influence social interaction and social policy.

Employing the two frames of Young's theoretical approach to oppression and justice and of disabilities studies, the oppression of women with disabilities can be seen as resulting primarily from practices, structures, and beliefs in society that reinforce negative stereotypes, curtail opportunities, promote violence, and marginalize them. This view does not, however, ignore the consequence of oppression on the psychic lives of women with disabilities. As a result of the internalization of these stigmatizing societal beliefs, women with disabilities have often come to expect from themselves what able-bodied or nonstigmatized individuals presuppose. Women with disabilities too often live in a nexus of public disgust and self-loathing. Degrading social treatment and denial of opportunities leads to a loss of self-worth and a disinterest in self-care. In order for change to become possible, we must raise the right-

[11] Young, *Justica and the Politics of Difference*, p.40.

eous lament. Young's experienced-based typology provides an outline for naming the group and individual accounts of oppression. I will define Young's terms, e.g., marginalization, exploitation, powerlessness, cultural imperialism, and violence, as I address them in the case of women with disabilities.

Marginalization

The findings of a recent Louis Harris poll are summarized as follows: 'being disabled ... means having much less education and money and ... less of almost everything in life than most other Americans'.[12] Young describes this type of oppression as marginalization, in which individuals are marked as useless to society as a whole and therefore prevented from participating in socially valued work.

Evidence of marginalization on the basis of disability is conclusive. People with disabilities are routinely excluded from paid employment. One study demonstrated that prospective employers ranked physically disabled individuals lower as prospective employees than all other minority groups, including senior citizens, student militants, and prison parolees.[13] Furthermore, two-thirds of the United States' population believe that people with disabilities are discriminated against in equal access to employment.[14]

These perceptions of discrimination are confirmed by work statistics. More than two-thirds of people with disabilities of working age are not working.[15] These staggering unemployment rates do not stem primarily from the lack of capacity or desire to work. Studies show that people with disabilities perform as well or bet-

[12] Louis Harris and Associates, *The ICD Survey of Disabled Americans: Bringing Disabled Americans into the Mainstream* (New York, International Center for the Disabled, 1986), p. 24.

[13] J. N. Colbert, R. A. Kalish, and P. Chang, 'Two Psychological Portals of Entry for Disadvantaged Groups', *Rehabilitation Literature,* 32 (1973), 194-201.

[14] Louis Harris and Associates, *Public Attitudes Toward People with Disabilities* (Washington, D.C., National Organization on Disability, 1991), p. 39.

[15] Louis Harris and Associates, *The ICD Survey of Disabled Americans.*

ter than able bodied co-workers, and more than 90 percent of people with disabilities want to work. A substantial minority of people with disabilities who are employed or willing and able to work confront discrimination, unfavorable attitudes, and physical barriers in the workplace. Three in 10 report encountering job discrimination.[16] Clearly disability results in workplace marginalization.

When marginalization occurs because of multiple stigmatized statuses, the effects are generally magnified. For example, white disabled men participate in the labor force at almost twice the rate of white disabled women (44 percent of men, only 24 percent of women). Disabled men are about half as likely as nondisabled men to work, whereas for white disabled women the gap is even greater, with disabled white women only three-eighths as likely to participate in the paid workforce as nondisabled white women. For African-Americans, the gender difference is far less significant: 26 percent of disabled men participate, as compared to 20 percent of disabled women. Across groups, fewer than 25 percent of women with disabilities participate in the labor force, and they are unemployed consistently more than are disabled men.[17]

Not only are women with disabilities marginalized in terms of paid workforce participation, but also in friendships and intimate partnerships. A study of friendship between disabled and nondisabled women notes that the nondisabled person's fear of the dependency of the disabled individual is a major barrier to intimacy.[18] Research further demonstrates that people with disabilities

---

[16] Louis Harris and Associates, *The ICD Survey of Disabled Americans*.

[17] A. Asch and M. Fine, 'Beyond Pedestals: Revisiting the Lives of Women with Disabilities' in M. Fine (ed.), *Disruptive Voices: The Possibilities of Feminist Research* (Ann Arbor, The University of Michigan Press, 1992), pp. 139-171.

[18] B. Fisher and R. Galler, 'Friendship and Fairness: How Disability Affects Friendship between Women' in M. Fine and A. Asch (eds.), *Women with Disabilities: Essays on Psychology, Culture and Politics* (Philadelphia, Temple University Press, 1988), pp. 172-194; see also F. Z. Belgrave and J. Mills, 'Effect upon Desire for Social Interaction with a Physically Disabled Person of Mentioning the Disability in Different Contexts', *Journal of Applied Social Psychology*, 11 (1981). 44-57; and J. O. Berry and W. H. Jones, 'Situations and Dispositional Components of Reactions toward Persons with Disabilities', *Journal of Social Psychology*, 131 (1991), 673-684.

are less likely than non-disabled people to be married, more likely
to marry later, and more likely to be divorced.[19] Moreover, while
both disabled men and women are perceived as inferior partners,
women with disabilities tend to be viewed more negatively by
both men and women than comparably disabled men.

Women with disabilities experience marginalization based on
gender and disability status. They are more marginalized than
either women without disabilities or men with disabilities, and
many are excluded from common spheres of social participation,
such as work, friendship, and intimate partnership.

Exploitation

Young describes exploitation as the 'steady process of the transfer of the results of the labor of one social group to benefit
another'.[20] Young illustrates her point by highlighting gender
exploitation in which two types of transfer occur, e.g., the transfer
of women's paid labor to men's advancement and the transfer of
nurturing and unpaid labor to the men's well-being. In the case of
women with disabilities, exploitation often takes the familiar
forms of gender exploitation. Employed disabled women tend to
be tracked in low-wage, service sectors.[21] The mean earnings of
disabled women fall far below those of disabled men. For both
disabled men and women, earnings are less than for their nondisabled counterparts.[22] As a result, women with disabilities have
more than twice the poverty rate of other United States' citizens.[23]

[19] From research by W.J. Hanna and B. Rogovsky, reported in Asch and Fine,
Disruptive Voices.

[20] Young, *Justice and the Politics of Difference*, p.49.

[21] See N. F. Russo and M. A. Jansen, 'Women, Work, and Disability: Opportunities and Challenges' in M. Fine and A. Asch, *Women with Disabilities,*
pp.229-244.

[22] Asch and Fine, *Beyond Pedestals*, p.149.

[23] J. M. McNeil, *Americans with Disabilities: 1991-1992*. United States
Bureau of the Census. Current Population Reports, P70-33 (Washington, D.C.,
United States Government Printing Office, 1993); S. N. Barnartt and J. B. Chris-
tiansen, 'The Socioeconomic Status of Deaf Workers: A Minority Group Perspective', *The Social Science Journal*, 22 (1985), 19-32.

Under-employment is also prevalent among women with disabilities. In general, people with disabilities are under-employed because the physically disabled are thought to be handicapped in their productive capacities and are 'seen to as social liabilities' in work settings.[24] Many are segregated in low-paying sheltered workshops, where they have little opportunity for advancement.[25] Experiences in such workshops and in the regular workplace show that frequently the benefits of their labor are not available to them.

Women with disabilities are not only systematically cut off from the profits of their work, they are also often denied the traditionally feminine work of nurturance and reproduction. A disabled woman's capacity to be a partner in an intimate, sexual relationship and her physical ability to conceive, bear, and rear children is often questioned. Attitudinal barriers and stereotypic perceptions of women with disabilities as asexual or sexually incapacitated either physically or emotionally severely restrict opportunities for intimate relationships. Asch and Fine contend that men spurn disabled women as workers and partners because they fail to measure up on grounds of appearance and of perceived abilities in physical and emotional caretaking.[26] Frequently a potential male partner feels he will be diminished in the eyes of other men if he can acquire only a substandard female partner. Additionally women with disabilities often find it difficult to remove themselves from abusive relationships because of physical dependence and lack of independent financial support.

Public abuse of women with disabilities who have chosen to be mothers has also been well documented.[27] For instance, in 1991 Bree Walker Lampley, a news broadcaster with ectrodactyly, was lampooned and abused on a call-in radio show for her decision to

---

[24] G. Best, 'The Minority Status of the Physically Disabled', *Cerebral Palsy Journal*, 28 (1967), 3.

[25] E. C. Wertlieb, 'Minority Group Status of the Disabled', *Human Relations*, 38 (1985), 1047-1063.

[26] Asch and Fine, *Beyond Pedestals*, p.19.

[27] M. Saxton, 'The Right to Bear Young: The Earl Hearing', *Disability Rag*, 14:3 (1994), 5-11.

have a child who would likely inherit her physical condition.[28] Other cases of public abuse of mothers with disabilities abound. Usually these cases exhibit stereotypes about the incompatibility of motherhood and physical disability.

The workplace experience of women with disabilities follows the familiar pattern of gender exploitation in which the benefits of their work are often appropriated by others. However, compared to able-bodied women, disabled women are much more likely to be relegated to the lowest paying jobs or in the case of some shelter workshops denied compensation entirely. Finally, women with disabilities are also likely to have fewer choices to pursue motherhood and marriage, and when they do they too frequently open themselves to private and public abuse.

Powerlessness

Young refers to the powerless as those who lack authority, status, and sense of self.[29] According to her, authority is a sanctioned right to make decisions. Influence, the aggregate of status and respectability, derives from expertise and opportunity. Thus the powerless who have no legitimate authority also cannot influence society.

A tangible evidence of powerlessness among women with disabilities is the typical educational status. Women with disabilities are five times as likely as able-bodied women to have fewer than eight years of schooling.[30] The relationship between educational attainment and disability is a complicated one. Women with little education are most likely to be in work or home situations that put them at risk for becoming disabled. For example, poverty not only

---

[28] Ectrodactyly is a congenital condition that results in the malformation of fingers and toes, which appear to be fused.

[29] Young, *Justice and the Politics of Difference*, p.57.

[30] Fine and Asch, *Women with Disabilities*, p.11; see also M. Davis and C. Marshall, 'Female and Disabled: Challenged Women in Education', *National Women's Studies Association Perspectives*, 5 (1987), 39-41.

correlates to lower education but also to at-risk status for disability, through such impairments as malnutrition and diabetes.

Additionally, girls with disabilities are much more likely to be kept away from or rendered powerless within educational institutions. One woman with a physical disability reports from her own experience of powerlessness. 'We were learning at a very early age that if you had a speech difficulty ... it was unlikely that you would successfully make it through the [school] system'.[31] She notes that teachers generally mistook slow speech as mental retardation and spent little time working directly with these students. Such autobiographical accounts of teacher bias and spread of judgment[32] are confirmed by researchers who found that terming a physically disabled student 'special', that is needing special education, consistently decreased teacher expectations for academic performance.[33] Given the disadvantages that accrue from being disabled and female, it is little wonder that women with disabilities are less likely than disabled men to have a college education.

Powerlessness continues when women with disabilities try to obtain medical care. Only half of persons with severe disabilities have private health insurance, and Medicare and Medicaid insure only about one-third of disabled people.[34] Torn between the need for independence and the need for adequate health care, women with disabilities are often forced to live with parents in order to maintain health insurance.

Furthermore, medical professionals often disregard the preferences and opinions of people with disabilities. Researchers have reported that medical doctors, rehabilitation nurses, and other

[31] S. Lonsdale, *Women and Disability: The Experience of Physical Disability among Women* (London, MacMillan Education, Ltd., 1990), p. 93.

[32] Spread of judgment occurs when individuals who are identified as having one disability are assumed to have other disabilities as well. For example, assumptions that a person who is deaf is also mentally retarded or that a wheelchair user is hard of hearing are evidence of spread of judgment.

[33] P. Schloss and S. R. Miller, 'Effects of the Labels 'Institutionalized' versus 'Regular School Student' on Teacher Expectations', *Exceptional Children*, 48:4 (1982), 361-362.

[34] McNeil, *Americans with Disabilities*; Shapiro, *No Pity*.

health care workers consistently underestimated the capabilities of people with physical disabilities, most particularly women.[35] Other findings note the relationship between the presence of a visible physical disability and judgments by health professionals. These medical professionals formed more favorable general impressions of individuals without a visible disability than for those with a disability. Least favorable impressions were reported for women with a visible disability and brash persons with visible disabilities.[36]

One of my most vivid memories from childhood was as a 10-year-old. A stop on medical rounds in a teaching hospital, my bed was circled by male medical students. One of them grabbed the corner of my crisp hospital sheet, whipping it away to reveal my naked body. As I lay humiliated at being naked, I realized that they weren't even looking at me. They noticed nothing but my fascinating wound. Ignorance of and disinterest in the experiences and concerns of those with disabilities can cause lasting psychic as well as physical damage. Too often we are powerless to prevent such abuse.

Without access to educational opportunities, women with disabilities are seldom able to ascend to positions of relative authority. Even within those realms, such as medical care, in which their roles as consumers should increase their authority, it often does not. Disabled women often receive inappropriate or inadequate medical treatment because of their powerlessness.

Cultural imperialism

The negative media images of women with disabilities as pitiable, passive creatures compounds their oppression. Young refers to cultural imperialism as the experience of people 'who find themselves

---

[35] C. De Loach and B. G. Greer, *Adjustment to Severe Physical Disability* (New York, McGraw-Hill, 1981); see also G. Albrecht, *The Disability Business* (Newbury Park, CA, SAGE, 1992).

[36] L. Gething, 'Judgments by Health Professionals of Personal Characteristics of People with a Visible Physical Disability', *Social Science and Medicine*, 34:7 (1992), 809-815.

defined from the outside, positioned, placed, by a network of dominant meanings they experience as arising from elsewhere, from
those with whom they do not identify and who do not identify with
them'.[37] Cultural imperialism refers to the reproduction of stereotypes that structure disability.

Stereotypes regarding people with disabilities are of two dominant types: (1) stereotypes that depict people with disabilities as
freaks or objects of fear and (2) stereotypes that depict people with
disabilities as inspirational or objects of pity.[38] Concerning the first
type, the preponderance of evidence suggests that persons with
physical disabilities are generally regarded as socially deviant and
feared by society.[39] This stereotype is often associated predominantly with disabled males. Film, television, and comics stereotype
men with disabilities, most often portraying them as villains, monsters, or self-pitying neurotics. Often these stereotypes present
them as individuals who display self-loathing and a keen desire for
revenge. For example, the Joker, Penguin, and Two-Face of *Batman, Batman Returns,* and *Batman Forever* fame are 'monsters'
whose evil deeds can be traced to their bitterness at being disabled.
Especially troubling in regard to this stereotype is the view that
physical disability causes or promotes social pathology.

Women with disabilities are also sometimes stereotyped as
frightening freaks. For example, the Grimm story 'Little Brother

---

[37] Young, *Justice and the Politics of Difference*, p.59.

[38] Shapiro, *No Pity*; I. Zola, 'Depictions of Disability: Metaphor, Message,
and Medium in the Research and Political Agenda', *Social Science Journal*, 22
(1985), 5-17; P. Longmore, 'Screening Stereotypes: Images of Disabled People',
Social Policy, 16 (1985), 31-37. Stereotypes about people with disabilities are not
limited to the two identified here. Haller identifies two other common stereotypical representations found in news stories, i.e., the medical model and the business
model. The medical model depicts people with disabilities as passively dependent
on health providers for maintenance and cure. The business model depicts people
with disabilities as costly to society and businesses in particular. These stereotypical representations while important, are not as widespread as those which perceive people with disabilities as freakish and objects of fear or inspirational and
objects of pity. See B. Haller, 'Rethinking Models of Media Representation of
Disability', *Disability Studies Quarterly*, 15 (1995), 26-30.

[39] S. Gazsi, *A Parallel and Imperfect Universe: The Media and People with
Disabilities* (New York, Columbia University Press, 1994); Longmore 1985.

and Little Sister' describes the bad girl as 'mean as a weasel and ugly and one-eyed as well'.[40] This disabled girl kills the virtuous queen in hopes of replacing her in the affections of the handsome king. A variation of this stereotype is revealed in the 1962 thriller 'What Ever Happened to Baby Jane?' in which Blanche Hudson (Joan Crawford) drove her sister Jane (Bette Davis) insane by allowing Jane to believe that she was responsible for the car accident that left Blanche crippled. Blanche had planned the car accident out of jealousy and made a miscalculation resulting in her own impairment. Stereotyped as devious and ugly, women with disabilities are bombarded with crippling images.

The second dominant stereotype depicts people with disabilities as inspirational or objects of pity. This, too, is a gendered stereotype often reserved for women with disabilities and children (who according to this stereotype are their functional equals). This stereotype is behind most television telethons. 'Jerry's Kids' on the annual Muscular Dystrophy Telethon – as well as numerous other telecasts – are smiling, cheery individuals whose pluck makes the tragedy of disability even more pitiable.[41] Portraying women with disabilities not only as pitiable but also as victims of their impairments is a common literary practice. Diane Price Herndl notes that novels and short stories by such writers as Edith Wharton, F. Scott Fitzgerald, and Edgar Allen Poe often represent an 'invalid ideology' of physically flawed, but virtuous womenhood.[42] Another example of this invalid ideology is Tennessee Williams' drama 'The Glass Menagerie' which depicts a disabled girl living in her fragile dream world. Represented as invalid and insubstantial, disabled women and girls are seen as victims and not agents.

---

[40] Reported in R. Thomson, 'Ann Petry's Mrs. Hedges and the Evil, One-eyed Girl: A Feminist Exploration of the Physically Disabled Female Subject', *Women's Studies*, 24 (1995), 599-614.

[41] Shapiro, *No Pity*; Fine and Asch, *Women with Disabilities*.

[42] D. P. Herndl, *Invalid Women: Figuring Feminine Illness in American Fiction and Culture, 1840-1940* (Chapel Hill, University of North Carolina Press, 1993). See also R. G. Thomson, *Extraordinary Bodies: Figuring Physical Disability in American Culture and Literature* (New York, Columbia University Press, 1997).

Cultural imperialism means that women with disabilities regularly encounter depictions that make the complexity and multiplicity of their experience invisible, replacing their lived reality with a one-dimensional cartoon. In accepting values and images of the dominant able-bodied femininity, women with disabilities can develop what W.E.B. DuBois called 'double consciousness', i.e., the split in personal evaluation and social depiction.[43] However, without support of a reference group of women with disabilities, cultural imperialism can result in internalization of societal messages of disabled women's inferiority and worthlessness. Acceptance of these beliefs makes women with disabilities vulnerable to abuse.

Violence

Young includes within the category of violence not only life-threatening incidents, but also harassment, intimidation, ridicule 'simply for the purpose of degrading, humiliating, or stigmatizing group members'.[44] No matter how it is defined, violence and abuse against people with disabilities is common. People with disabilities are one and a half times more likely to experience at least one incident of physical abuse than are able-bodied individuals.[45] Rates of severe, multiple victimizations of children with disabilities are twice as high as for the general population.[46] In a study of Canadian women, researchers found that physical abuse of women

[43] W. E. B. DuBois, *The Souls of Black Folk* (New York, Modern Library, [1953] 1996).

[44] Young, *Justice and the Politics of Difference*, p.61.

[45] D. Sobsey, *Violence and Abuse in the Lives of People with Disabilities: The End of Silent Acceptance?* (Baltimore, Paul H. Brooks Publishing Co., 1994); D. Sobsey and C. Varnhagen, 'Sexual Abuse, Assault, and Exploitation of Individuals with Disabilities' in C. Bagley and R. J. Thomlinson (eds.), *Child Sexual Abuse: Critical Perspectives on Prevention, Intervention, and Treatment* (Toronto, Ontario, Canada, Center for Human Development and Research, 1991), pp. 201-216.

[46] See Sobsey, *Violence and Abuse*; H. Westcott, 'The Abuse of Disabled Children: A Review of the Literature', *Child Care, Health, and Development*, 17 (1991), 243-258.

with disabilities was double that recorded among able-bodied women.[47] Given higher rates of abuse of women generally in the United States, it is reasonable to speculate that this ratio is applicable in United States' society as well. Particularly disturbing about these findings is that most abuse is perpetrated against women with disabilities by family members, care-givers, or health-care professionals.[48] Battered and humiliated by those closest to them, women with disabilities often suffer for years with no outside intervention.

According to Young, the presence of any one of the five faces of oppression – marginalization, exploitation, powerlessness, cultural imperialism, and violence – is sufficient to call a group oppressed. Women with disabilities are unquestionably oppressed in American society. Objectified and invisible, beaten and exploited, we are simply 'things not seen' to most able-bodied people.

Reflecting theologically on the oppression of women with disabilities

Whenever I reflect theologically on the oppression of women with disabilities, I by necessity face my own history. I have long been involved in the disability rights movement seeking to better the situation of women with disabilities. I have also been a life-long Christian in various denominations and among quite divergent local communities. For much of my life, I experienced a significant rift between my participation in the disability rights movement and my Christian faith. The movement offered opportunities for social action that were largely unavailable in my Christian context, but my faith gave me a spiritual fulfillment that I found elusive in the movement. The movement strengthened my capacity for lamentation, but offered few sources of sustaining hope; whereas the hope available in too many Christian commu-

---

[47] J. Doucette, *Violent Acts against Disabled Women* (Toronto, Ontario, Canada, DisAbled Women's Network Canada, 1986).
[48] Fine and Asch, *Women with Disabilities*, p.22.

nities seemed a meager offering, when my lamentations were unwelcome.

Through reflecting critically on my work within the disability rights movement and by returning again to the biblical message, I began to reconcile my two worlds and encountered the Disabled God. The initial encounter happened in the Shepherd Spinal Center in Atlanta – a rehabilitation hospital for people with spinal cord injuries. I had been asked by the facility's chaplain to lead a Bible study with several residents. For several weeks, the study had been plodding along without much enthusiasm on my part and even less on the part of the other participants. One afternoon after a long and frustrating day, I shared with the group my doubts about God's care for me. I asked them if they could tell me how they would know that God was with them and understood their experiences. A long silence ensued; then an African-American young man with quadriplegia[49] said, 'If God was in a sip/puff [wheelchair] maybe he would understand.' The afternoon session concluded without much discussion of the image.

Several weeks later, as I read the Gospel passage from Luke 24:36-39, I started with recognition. The account is of Jesus' followers who are alone and depressed. The resurrected Jesus appears urging his followers to touch the crucifixion wounds as evidence that he was the risen Christ. Reading this passage, I came to realize that the foundation of Christian theology is the resurrection of Jesus Christ; but seldom is the resurrected Christ recognized as a deity whose hands, feet, and side bear the marks of profound physical impairment. The resurrected Christ of our tradition is a disabled God. This Disabled God understood the experience of those in my Shepherd Center Bible study as well as my own.

In the years since that initial encounter I have sought to correlate the encounter with the Disabled God and my ongoing reflection on the social situation of women with disabilities. The liberatory theology that continues to emerge is driven by the need to lament the social conditions under which we live and to work to

---

[49] Quadriplegia is paralysis of both arms and both legs.

transform societies that oppress us. Justice for women with disabilities necessitates that equal access to employment be an ongoing social priority. It also requires that we commit ourselves to promotion of human flourishing by listening carefully to the vocational callings of those around us – disabled and temporarily able-bodied – and by mobilizing our resources to assist one another to find meaningful work in the world.

A liberatory theology of disability necessitates that we subject our personal affinities to the call of Christ to right action. When I speak with groups of women with disabilities, I often hear the desire for intimate sexual and filial love. The pain of isolation and lack of intimacy is frequently acute. In the face of these calls for intimacy, what does justice demand? Although this will be particular to each person, justice demands that we uncover our aversions and biases about people with disabilities. In theological settings, we must speak openly about the sexism and revulsion against people with disabilities that is endemic in society. Critical reflection on the situation of women with disabilities leads us to a call for moral accountability for our attitudes that result in the isolation of those whom we deem unworthy of hospitality and friendship. A liberatory theology of disability necessitates that women with disabilities are known not according to the skewed visions of stereotypes, but rather in all our particularity. We must unname these damaging images and claim ourselves as made fully in the image of God. Just as African-Americans have spoken out opposing the damaging representations of themselves as pimps, hustlers, and prostitutes in the media, so, too, must people with disabilities and others who care resist the crippling images delivered to them in popular culture.

While just action is vital to the flourishing of people with disabilities and the temporarily able-bodied, it is not enough. As our analysis of stereotypes showed, the injustice experienced by women with disabilities is not simply a matter of deliberate institutional and individual discrimination, though it is unquestionably that; it is also a matter of values, ideas, and images that permeate the webs of meaning that inform people's lives. These resources that people draw on in making sense of their own and other lives are, implicitly if not explicitly, saturated with religious meaning. These religious meanings address our deepest concerns and give purpose to our ordinary lives. New religious images, ideas, and values about disability are essential as we seek to live our ordinary lives. Without them, the barriers that women with disabilities encounter while they may occasionally be lowered, will never be demolished.

I want to mention four implications of practical theological reflection on the social situation of women with disabilities, raising the lament, and encountering the Disabled God. The first is the theological task of re-reading and unreading biblical narrative in light of the experience of people with disabilities; the second identifies the theological meaning of difference; the third highlights dangers of utopianism; and the fourth underscores the need for a risky imagination in the theological work of lamentation and transformation of the lives of women with disabilities.

First, new strategies for critical interpretation of the biblical story are vital for transforming ideas and images about women with disabilities. Feminist biblical scholars must re-read the texts not only for understanding the role of gender in their interpretation but also to identify the treatment of women we would now name disabled and their caregivers. New Testament scholar Gail O'Day has contributed to this work in her analysis of Matthew's account of the Canaanite woman's petition to Jesus for her daughter who is 'severely possessed by a demon' (15:22). O'Day highlights the similarity between the rhetorical structure of the woman's words and the narrative enactment of a lament psalm. O'Day states her interpretation: 'The Canaanite woman stands fully in the tradition of Abraham and Moses who were not afraid to bargain with God (Gn 18:22-23; Nm 11:11-15); she is profoundly linked with all the broken and needy petitioners who sang Israel's songs of lament, with all those who cling to the faithfulness to the promise'.[50] We

---

[50] G. O'Day, 'Surprised by Faith: Jesus and the Canaanite Woman,' *Listening: Journal of Religion and Culture*, 24 (1989), p. 299. See also E. Schüssler Fiorenza, *But She Said: Feminist Practices of Biblical Interpretation* (Boston, Beacon Press, 1992).

have glimpses from biblical accounts of the actions and responses of people who have suffered because of disability. Yet there is much to be done.

Second, women with disabilities enable the Christian community to rethink the meaning of difference in its midst. Our presence reminds everyone that the boundaries of group difference are ambiguous and shifting, without clear borders. Individuals who are currently able-bodied have a greater than 50 percent chance of becoming physically disabled, either temporarily or permanently. Understanding the fluid boundaries marking difference and sameness can then facilitate coalitions rather than support group essentialism. Ours is the only minority you can join involuntarily, without warning, at any time. For many temporarily able bodies, our bodies in trouble predict their future and urge them to confront these radical transformations. Difference as a theological category names us to ourselves. We have yet fully to encounter what we may also become.

Third, theological reflection on the concrete situations of women with disabilities raises again the dangers of utopian theological analysis. Women with disabilities have learned that teaching a compromise with bodies and others who care is a slow, painful process in which our legitimate needs sometimes press hard against real limits. Resisting the utopias of the human body envisioned in popular culture which constructs body-built monuments of muscle or the towers of strength and stamina of high-performance athletes as normal requires that we acknowledge the God-given limits of our bodies.

The struggle to attend to limits while calling for self and societal transformation is an ongoing challenge for those who work for justice. Theological analysis of disability is one of the few remaining areas where theologians and religious professionals in good conscience tell people to defer their flourishing until the afterworld. This theological utopianism is a siren song that too often drowns out our real and necessary calls for justice and the possibility of human flourishing within the limits of our real lives. Accepting limits as God-given means facing the divine in our imperfect bodies with all their pains and conundrum; it also means risking a new vision of God.

I have a friend, Alice Wexler, who is at risk for the genetic disease Huntington's.[51] The disease strikes people in the mid-40s usually and results in a prolonged, progressive loss of mental and nervous capacity. Alice watched her mother die a long and painful death from Huntington's disease. She and her sister worked hard to enable scientists to find the genetic marker for the condition. After nearly a decade, the genetic marker was found and a test was devised to enable people at risk to know positively if they carried the gene, and thus whether or not they would develop the disease – since to have the gene was to be certain of having the disease. After she had worked for the test, Alice decided not to take it herself. She explained her choice by telling me that she could flourish with a risk, but no matter if the test was positive or negative she would find it difficult to reconcile herself to no risk when so many with whom she struggled were at risk still.

Being at risk is the fundamental experience of human life. The theological use we make of this is up to us. By cultivating a risky imagination we open new possibilities for being in the world. Ethicist Sharon Welch writes: 'The fundamental risk constitutive of this ethic is the decision to care and to act although there are no guarantees of success. Such action requires immense daring and enables deep joy'.[52] We must develop and cultivate a risky ethical and theological imagination that asks and begins to answer what is God's vision for human flourishing – not just for some but for all, not just for the able-bodied but for the disabled, not just for men but for women, not just the Western world but for the entire world. For some simply encountering the Disabled God is sufficiently risky. However, I believe that this encounter can open at least the possibility for conceiving the ways God is already acting in the world and for developing new and better

---

[51] A. Wexler, *Mapping Fate: A Memoir of Family, Risk, and Genetic Research* (New York, Times Books, 1995).

[52] See S. D. Welch, *A Feminist Ethic of Risk* (Minneapolis, Fortress Press, 1990), p. 68.

visions for the church that must risk itself in order to see justice enacted.

I am convinced that if we raise the lamentations of women with disabilities, look carefully and critically at our religious traditions, encounter the Disabled God, and develop a risky theological imagination, we can begin to transform the lives of women with disabilities and to challenge temporarily able bodied women and men who glimpse a new understanding of themselves, the world around, and the God who is with them in new and risky ways.

ADDITIONAL BIBLIOGRAPHY

Avalos, Hector. *Illness and Health Care in the Ancient Near East: The Role of the Temple in Greece, Mesopotamia, and Israel*, Harvard Semitic Monographs, no. 54, Atlanta, Scholars Press, 1995

Bishop, Marilyn E.(ed.). *Religion and Disability: Essays in Scripture, Theology, and Ethics*, Kansas City, Sheed and Ward, 1994

Black, Kathy. *A Healing Homiletic: Preaching and Disability*, Nashville, Abingdon Press, 1996

Browne, Susan, Connors, Debra and Stern, Nanci (eds.). *With the Power of each Breath: A Disabled Women's Anthology*, Pittsburgh, Cleis Press, 1985

Cooper, Burton. 'The Disabled God', *Theology Today*, 49:2 (1992), 173-82

DeVries, Dawn. 'Creation, Handicapism and the Community of Differing Abilities' in R. S. Chopp and M. L. Taylor (eds.), *Reconstructing Christian Theology*, Minneapolis, Fortress, 1994

Disability Studies Quarterly. Religion, Spirituality, and Disability Issue, *Disability Studies Quarterly*, 15:3 (1995)

Eiesland, Nancy. *The Disabled God: Toward a Liberatory Theology of Disability*, Nashville, Abingdon Press, 1994

Eiesland, Nancy and Saliers, Don (eds.). *Human Disability and the Service of God: Theological Perspectives on Disability*, Nashville, Abingdon Press, forthcoming

Foley, Edward (ed.). *Developmental Disabilities and Sacramental Access: New Paradigms for Sacramental Encounters*, Collegeville, MN, Liturgical Press, 1994

Fontaine, Carole. 'Disabilities and Illness in the Bible: A Feminist Perspective' in Athalya Brenner (ed.), *Feminist Companion to the New Testament*, Sheffield, Sheffield Academic Press, 1995

Govig, Stewart. *Strong at the Broken Places: Persons with Disabilities and the Church*, Louisville, Westminster/John Knox Press, 1989

Lane, Nancy. 'Healing Bodies and Victimization of Persons: Issues of Faith-healing for Persons with Disabilities', *The Disability Rag Resource*, 14:3 (1993), 11-13

Mairs, Nancy. *Ordinary Time: Cycles in Marriage, Faith and Renewal*, Boston, Beacon Press, 1993

National Organization on Disability. *That All May Worship: An Interfaith Welcome to People with Disabilities*, Washington, D.C., National Organization on Disability, 1994

—. *Loving Justice: The ADA and the Religious Community*, Washington, D.C., National Organization on Disability, 1994

Pailin, David. *A Gentle Touch: From a Theology of Handicap to a Theology of Human Being*, London, SPCK, 1992

Ransom, Judy Griffith. *The Courage to Care: Seven Congregations are Transformed by Reaching Out to Families with Disabilities*, Nashville, Upper Room Books, 1994

Webb-Mitchell, Brett. *God Plays Piano, Too: The Spiritual Lives of Disabled Children*, New York, Crossroads, 1994

—. *Unexpected Guests at God's Banquet: Welcoming People with Disabilities into the Church*, New York, Crossroads, 1994

Young, Frances. *Face to Face: A Narrative Essay in the Theology of Suffering*, Edinburgh, T. & T. Clark, 1990

VII

A view from a room: feminist practical theology[1] from academy, kitchen or sanctuary?

Elaine GRAHAM

Introduction: beyond sexism and clericalism

In this article, I want to reflect on certain general social and religious dimensions which shape Christian ministry and practical theology in Britain today: issues of secularization, pluralism and the changing role of women. I shall do so from the vantage-point of my own context as a woman academic in an urban university in Northern England. I will continue by discussing how a feminist practical theology is actually emerging out of Christian feminist *praxis*. The story of one particular 'woman-church' community – the St. Hilda community – which serves both the pastoral and liturgical needs of its members, will illustrate my argument. I conclude by arguing that feminist practical theology emerges from the encounter between faith and practice in the form of the values embodied and enacted in the diversity of pastoral responses to women's changing needs and perspectives. In the development of a feminist practical theology in Britain, it has been crucial to counter the invisibility of women. The stimulus for my own initial

---

[1] In a British context the terms 'pastoral theology' and 'practical theology' are often used interchangeably. I shall use the term 'practical theology' for purposes of consistency with other contributors. My own understanding would regard practical theology as the critical study of the theological values which underpin and inform a diversity of Christian practices, extending beyond the activities of pastoral care and counselling to encompass preaching, Christian formation, spiritual direction, liturgy and congregational studies.

researches in practical theology was the churches' pastoral neglect
of much of the fabric of women's lives. Women's experiences of
motherhood, work, ageing, caring and inequality, not to mention
their attempts to realize a vocation to the Christian ministry, were
notably absent from the pastoral care tradition.

My subsequent examination of the pastoral care literature of the
modern period in Europe and North America revealed that the
exclusion of women was deeply entrenched in the tradition.[2] Until
the first quarter of the twentieth-century, women were excluded
from the ordained ministry in most Christian denominations in
Britain. By virtue of their lay standing, women were deemed
unqualified to undertake any kind of ministry or pastoral care; yet,
in reality, many women did exercise significant pastoral tasks
while maintaining successful professional careers. Such contributions were afforded little status; Christian pastoral care was
equated with clerical definitions of ministry, thereby devaluing
anything not carried out by the clergy.

Some of the pastoral care literature of this period did feature
women as the recipients of pastoral care; but the overwhelming
focus on the activities of the pastoral *agent* meant that the experiences and perspectives of the pastoral *client* were afforded little
authority. In the few discussions of the pastoral needs of women,
they tended to be characterized in stereotypical form, as neurotic,
dependent and unstable.

The effect of these 'clericalist' and 'sexist' paradigms was to
establish a tradition of practical theology which operated from the
perspective of the male, ordained pastor; one in which any kind
of 'client-centred' commitment was unknown. The genesis of a
feminist practical theology begins with the exposure and critique
of such an androcentric tradition.[3] However, it cannot stop there.
'Critique' must necessarily be followed by the task of 'reconstruction'. Accounts of pastoral care which take women's experi-

---

[2] E.L. Graham, 'The Pastoral Needs of Women', *Contact: The Interdisciplinary Journal of Pastoral Studies*, 100 (1989), 23-25.
[3] E.L. Graham, 'Pastoral Theology, Feminism and the Future', *Contact: the
Interdisciplinary Journal of Pastoral Studies*, 103 (1990), 2-9.

ences seriously and value them as givers *and* receivers of care, challenge exclusive and prescriptive definitions and set out a more authentic picture of the diversity of methods and contexts of Christian ministry.

Speaking from a context

Looking out from my office at the University I see a cherry tree in full blossom. At the time of writing, in late spring, the tree is at its most magnificent, although the rain showers quickly dampen its splendour and scatter the pink petals like confetti.

I am lucky to have such a spectacular tree outside my room; most of the rest of the campus is stone, concrete and red brick, and it straddles one of the busiest main roads into Manchester city centre. Apart from my garden enclave, therefore, this is a very urban context. It is also one of the largest higher education complexes in the Western world: a network of institutions dedicated to the pursuit of intellectual excellence. The mock Gothic buildings reflecting the University's Victorian origins are now surrounded by computing, science and engineering labs, their plate glass exteriors adding to their inscrutability. In one older building is the room where the first computer was built (in the 1940s these prototypes filled a room the size of a lecture theatre). A few blocks away is the laboratory where Rutherford first split the atom.

From the second floor of my building I can look out over the University campus to the areas known as Moss Side and Hulme, two of the most economically disadvantaged areas in Britain, and graphic testimonies to urban decline and social polarization. The landscape of these areas has been dramatically altered in the past few years. The once-lauded social housing experiments of the 1960s are steadily being demolished, replaced by new 'model' housing developments, the result of partnership between the City Council and local business. This is 1990s social policy, in which any talk of social engineering to end inequality has been replaced by the more cautious rhetoric of 'Urban Regeneration'.[4]

Today the headline in the newspaper reads, 'The End of the Welfare State'.[5] For anyone involved in health and welfare provision or for those concerned as consumers of education, medical care, housing, local social services or income support, such a verdict confirms what we all already feared: the State, funded by public taxation and expenditure, can no longer be relied upon to bear the primary burden of support for those in need, or to intervene as a vehicle of social change.

Such a withdrawal from interventionist or social democratic policies is a legacy of eighteen years of Conservative government, in which the values of individualism, free enterprise and competitiveness were prized, and the functions and responsibilities of government were reduced to a minimum. The people of Hulme and Moss Side bear the real burden of such policies, as social polarization grows and social commentators speak of a decay of communities and the growth of an increasingly alienated 'underclass'.[6]

Many of my students live and work in areas like Moss Side and Hulme: in East Manchester, Stockport, Liverpool, Leeds and right across the North-West of England. The stories of such areas, prone to disproportionate incidence of poverty, unemployment, ill-health and crime, form the subtext for our scholarly discussions. But they are stories in which hope leavens the despair. In many areas, the

---

[4] *Manchester – 50 Years of Change: Post-War Planning in Manchester* (London, HMSO, 1995), pp. 93-102.

[5] *Guardian* (Manchester and London), Wednesday May 8 1996, p. 1.

[6] The Commission on Social Justice, *Social Justice: Strategies for National Renewal* (London, Vintage, 1994); Manchester Health for All Working Party, *Health Inequalities and Manchester in the 1990s* (Manchester City Council, 1993). Indicators of differentials in income and of poverty suggest that social inequality in Britain has increased in the past fifteen years. For example, in 1979, one child in ten lived in poverty; in 1993, the proportion was one in three (Commission on Social Justice, *Social Justice*, p. 31). Other social research suggests that women are especially vulnerable to the factors that contribute to poverty: low pay, job insecurity, family dependents, old age: see C. Glendenning and J. Millar (eds.), *Women and Poverty in Britain in the 1990s* (Hemel Hempstead, Harvester Wheatsheaf, 1992).

church remains the only major organized body of the statutory or
voluntary sectors to maintain its buildings and services. It therefore acts as a focus of community organization and endeavour, and
the Christian community is valued for its willingness to 'keep
faith' with the inner cities.[7]

Frequently, the stories of inner city communities feature leading
roles for women. Church involvement in Greater Manchester has
focused on the support of Credit Unions, voluntary (and locally-
run) associations in which money is collectively saved and lent
independent of big business or local loan sharks. Women are
prominent in such groups, as organizers and clients, and thereby
take a prominent role in actively creating and generating the hope
and mutual reliance which are so vital for survival.[8]

Such stories, and many more like them, offer our academic discussions a necessary focus. The central issue is essentially about
the relationship between faith and values on the one hand, and collective and individual action on the other. Whether this be the theological convictions which impel the churches to denounce government policies on housing, immigration or unemployment, or
the religious roots of politicians' 'conviction politics',[9] such
debates remind us that economic and social policies which shape

[7] The British churches have maintained a constant flow of reports and programmes related to the plight of the inner cities. The best known of these is The
Archbishop's Commission on Urban Priority Areas, *Faith in the City* (London,
Church Information Office, 1985), which brought the Church into open conflict
with the Thatcher government, and which put paid to the description of the
Church of England as 'the Conservative party at prayer'. For a fuller (and critical)
account of this, see H. Clark, *The Church Under Thatcher* (London, SPCK, 1992).

[8] R. Jenkins, *Women and Poverty in Salford* (Manchester, William Temple
Foundation, 1989), gives an account of various women's initiatives in Salford,
Greater Manchester.

[9] Margaret Thatcher was the epitome of such a concept. It is said that her
values of self-reliance and individualism derived from a strict evangelical Protestant upbringing. Interestingly, the current (1997) Labour Prime Minister, Tony
Blair, also attributes his political formation to Christian values: in his case, the
Scottish communitarian philosopher John Macmurray. Despite the secular nature
of British society, therefore, religion still represents a significant factor in public
moral and political discourse. See M. Allison (ed.), *Christianity and Conservatism*
(London, Hodder & Stoughton, 1990); C. Bryant (ed.), *Reclaiming the Ground:
Christianity and Socialism* (London, Hodder & Stoughton, 1993).

the life of the nation often derive from ethical and religious beliefs and world-views.

Our practical theology programme at Manchester therefore traces the origins of notions of citizenship, participation and community which underly the changing horizon and fabric of inner-city Manchester. We examine the religious values and beliefs which have shaped the churches' intervention in social and political debates, and which inform the everyday relationships and interactions between church and community. We explore how the theological tradition of humanity created in the image of God might inspire the values of Christian ministry. And we ask how patterns of individual pastoral care and social action serve as the 'incarnation' of the truth-claims of Christian theology.

Religion, culture and gender in contemporary Britain

However, other aspects of life in Britain decisively shape the context within which practical theology is conducted. It may come as a surprise to some readers if I say that Britain is a very secular society. This statement has to be qualified, of course: religious behaviour and affiliation is by no means uniform in Britain today. But practical theologians must take their context seriously; and one feature which strikes any observer of the British scene is the steady decline in long-established religious institutions. Whilst the origins and causes of such decline are still hotly debated, it is broadly the case that the mainstream Christian denominations are losing active members at an unprecedented rate.[10] The same is true of Anglo-Jewry, whose numerical decline is causing significant anxiety and comment.[11]

[10] G. Davie, *Religion in Britain since 1945: Believing without Belonging* (Oxford, Blackwell, 1994).

[11] D. Englander, 'Integrated but insecure: a portrait of Anglo-Jewry at the close of the twentieth century' in G.Parsons (ed.), *The Growth of Religious Diversity: Britain from 1945* (London, Routledge, 1993), pp. 95-131; J. Sacks, *Will we have Jewish Grandchildren? Jewish Continuity and how to achieve it* (London, Vallentine Mitchell, 1994).

Yet the precise religious contours of British society are sometimes hard to trace. Despite such low levels of formal participation in the Christian churches, the vast majority of Britons still retain a degree of informal, non-denominational, religious sentiment. Studies consistently reveal that two-thirds of interviewed samples express a belief in God, with significant proportions admitting to regular times of prayer.[12] The so-called 'Celtic fringes' of the North of Ireland, Wales and Scotland also display a stronger persistence of formal church-going than urban England.[13] This is the context in which practical theology is conducted, and it is important to remember that formal religious affiliation is a minority interest amidst a non-participating, but nevertheless religiously sympathetic, population.

If Britain is no longer a Christian country – even if not quite a *post*-Christian one – due to the decline in formal participation, then the presence of ethnic minorities is also an important feature of our current context. The British Empire may well have been dismantled finally in the years immediately after 1945; but a colonial past has endured in the political, economic and cultural ties between Britain and Africa, the Caribbean and South Asia. The result has been the establishment of many ethnic minority communities within Britain, and has introduced the reality of religious and cultural *pluralism* into contemporary life.[14] Of most significance has been the growing prominence of British Islam – there are now well over a million Muslims in Britain – and the troubled relationship between Afro-Caribbean Christians and the 'white-majority' churches, a matter to which I shall return later.[15] Whilst the importance of British cultural, ethnic and religious pluralism is

[12] A. Greeley, 'Religion in Britain, Ireland and USA' *British Social Attitudes*, 9th Report 1992/3 (Brighton, Gower, 1993).

[13] Davie, *Religion in Britain since 1945*, pp. 94-105.

[14] G. Parsons (ed.), *The Growth of Religious Diversity: Britain from 1945*, Vol. II: *Issues* (London, Routledge, 1993), Intro-duction; R. Ballard (ed.), *Desh Pardesh: the South Asian Presence in Britain* (London, Hurst & Co., 1994).

[15] P. Lewis, *Islamic Britain: Religion, Politics and Identity among British Muslims* (London, I.B. Tauris, 1994); J.L. Wilkinson, *Church in Black and White* (Edinburgh, St. Andrew Press, 1993).

potentially very significant for society and the churches, most branches of contemporary theology, including British feminist Christian theology, have largely failed to reflect a context in which the primacy of Christianity can no longer be taken for granted.

Christian feminism and the church

The changing role of women in the British churches cannot be fully appreciated outside the historical development of Western feminism. The women's movement in Britain owes most of its impetus to the broader campaigns of socialism and trade unionism, and to self-consciously woman-identified programmes such as women's refuges, abortion reform and cultural feminism. The religious underpinning of early feminist activism has, however, been underplayed. Until recently, the academic study of feminism reflected an overwhelming hostility to religion. Christian feminism in Britain struggles against isolation within the women's movement as well as lack of acceptance within the churches.[16]

Today, women's calls for change resound throughout society. These calls are now being augmented by voices from the Christian community in the shape of Christian feminists of all denominations and backgrounds. Some choose to work for change within the institutional churches, whilst others locate themselves beyond the religious structures in order to pursue a new kind of spiritual quest for women.[17] Women have achieved some degree of recog-

---

[16] The gulf between academic feminist scholarship and feminist theology in Britain is a seriously neglected issue. I have attempted to address this question in 'Feminist Theology: Myth, Mystery or Monster?' in Liz Stanley (ed.), *Knowing feminisms* (London and California, Sage Publications, 1997).

[17] Daphne Hampson is the best-known British feminist theologian/philosopher to argue that feminism and Christianity are incompatible. Her journey through the campaign for women's ordination in the Anglican tradition towards a more 'post-Christian' spirituality is recorded in *Theology and Feminism* (Oxford, Blackwell, 1990). For an extended debate between British feminist theologians of varying perspectives, see D. Hampson, (ed.), *Swallowing a Fishbone? Feminist Theologians Debate Christianity* (London, SPCK, 1996).

nition in the free church (Protestant) traditions; but the prospects in the Roman Catholic Church look as bleak as ever. There are a number of pressure groups for women's ministry in the Roman Catholic Church but I suspect that many women and progressive lay men have chosen to channel their energies into world development and peace and justice campaigns out of sheer frustration at ever shifting the institution on its conservative stance towards women's wider participation.[18]

Any discussion of women and the church, and especially questions of ministry and practical theology, is inevitably dominated by the question of women's ordination to the priesthood in the Church of England, a campaign which ran from the mid-1970s until the early 1990s. It was an epic struggle and defined so much of the preoccupations and priorities of Christian feminism during the 1970s and 1980s.[19] Many Christian feminists would admit to some ambivalence at the pre-eminence of this one issue during this period. For example, media coverage focused on the novelty of women priests in the Anglican context at the expense of acknowledging the existence of women ministers in other denominations, let alone examining their achievements and problems. Similarly, sections of the women's movement in the churches remained robustly laicized, and resented the suggestion (as they saw it) that Christian feminism might simply be equated with equal opportunities for women in the priesthood, thereby avoiding wider questions about the nature of ministry and leadership in the churches. Nevertheless, the campaign for the ordination of women in the Established Church served as an important focus for mobilizing many women and men; and although many did not move beyond the single issue of priesthood (and actively eschewed any association with feminist theology) many others were radicalized

---

[18] D. McEwan (ed.), *Women Experiencing Church: a documentation of alienation* (Leominster, Gracewing, 1991).

[19] S. Dowell and J. Williams (eds.), *Bread, wine and women: the ordination debate in the Church of England* (London, Virago, 1994); J. Field-Bibb, *Women Towards Priesthood: Ministerial Praxis and Feminist Politics* (Cambridge, Cambridge University Press, 1991).

by the experience into further exploration of more overtly feminist issues.[20]

The struggle of women in church and society is therefore a major factor informing my activities as a professional practical theologian. Local factors, once again, shape my story. The University of Manchester was the first institution in Britain to offer undergraduate or graduate programmes in feminist theology. Like any good religion, feminist theology at Manchester has its own myth of origin. The legend goes that a prestigious (male) guest lecturer spoke of feminist theology as 'taking the whingeing[21] out of the kitchen and into the seminar room'. The resulting outcry culminated in the first version of the course (launched in 1986 and entitled 'Women, Men and Christian Theology') which I continue to teach to this day.

At one level, of course, this description was a typically patriarchal insult, suggesting that women in the academy could never properly shed their domestic preoccupations. Ironically, though, I am also aware of a great deal of 'kitchen table theology' taking place within British Christian feminism, insofar as theology is discussed and practised in contexts which extend well beyond the confines of the academy. In Manchester we have attempted to straddle the boundary between academic and popular theology by running regular 'Saturday Schools' in Feminist Theology, which are organized and run by graduate students and open to the public as part of the University's continuing education provision.

Such an approach recognizes that a university course or qualification is but one amongst many routes into, and expressions of, feminist theological commitment, and that academic endeavour must be accountable to a wider community. The context and conviviality of the (metaphorical) kitchen table, as well as the rarefied air of the academy, are thus acknowledged and affirmed as legiti-

---

[20] See Dowell and Williams (eds.), *Bread, Wine and Women*, pp. 49-58. For a discussion of the experiences of women deacons in the Church of England prior to the 1992 vote, see C. Treasure, *Walking on Glass: Women Deacons Speak Out* (London, SPCK, 1991).

[21] Whining, complaining.

mate starting-points for our theologizing.[22] This amounts to an alternative feminist epistemology, crucial to the development of a feminist practical theology: starting with experience, it also seeks to integrate the values of affectivity, justice and care with those of rationality and agency.[23] We need, however, also to be wary of over-romanticizing the kitchen context, in case it communicates another kind of domestic captivity for women. Feminists speak of privileging and articulating women's experience, but there is a danger of re-stereotyping the perspectives from which women speak. We may wish to claim the right to have our kitchen table recognized as a site of legitimate theological work, to see the world of nurture and family as important vantage-points from which to locate theological insights: for it is, after all, where many women do the bulk of their pastoral care. Economic reality also dictates that many women write at their kitchen tables because they cannot gain research grants or high-status university positions. A celebration of the experiential and informal roots of Christian feminism must not, however, be used as a device to imprison women in a domestic space or deny them access to academic excellence and wider opportunities. Women also have to insist on their right to take their legitimate places in the seminar room, the lecture theatre and the laboratory.

The many local Christian feminist groups meeting in kitchens, sitting rooms and church halls are therefore a vital part of the contemporary feminist theological scene. It would be mistaken, however, to regard these informal groups as merely the consumers of feminist theologies which are actually generated elsewhere. Such groups are also the producers and originators of important and

---

[22] For examples of feminist theology which seeks to integrate the experiential and the conventionally academic, see: L. Russell et al. (eds.), *In Search of our Mother's Gardens* (Philadelphia, Westminster, 1985); The Mud Flower Collective, *God's Fierce Whimsy: Christian Feminism and Theological Education* (New York, Pilgrim Press, 1985).

[23] One example of attempts to construct a feminist way of knowing derived from everyday relationships and activities of work, care and experience may be found in H. Rose, *Love, power and knowledge: towards a feminist transformation of the sciences* (Cambridge, Polity Press, 1994.)

vital work. They are in fact the sources for an alternative epistemology for feminist practical theology: they are spaces in which
diverse experiences and ways of knowing may be articulated.

Feminist theology and feminist praxis

Christian feminists are often accused by religious opponents of
falling prey to 'secular' ideologies concerning women's liberation.
Such a view assumes that those gullible enough to embrace the
divisive and confrontational world-view of feminism are automat-
ically abandoning their Christian principles in favour of a purely
secular creed.[24] Yet this perspective ignores the decisive links
between nineteenth-century first-wave feminism and Christianity
in Britain and the United States.[25] It also implicitly precludes
Christians from acknowledging the presence of God at work
within social or philosophical movements other than Christianity.

By contrast, I would argue that feminist theological critiques of
androcentricism and hierarchy in the Christian tradition, and the
reconstruction of more inclusive visions, are not merely motivated
by secular feminism. The practical endeavours of feminist theologians to create more authentic and inclusive communities and ministries are informed by a vision of transcendence, justice and hope
which is actually profoundly *theological*.

A recent volume of essays on women and pastoral care, entitled
Life-Cycles, was the first attempt to articulate an agenda for practical theology informed by feminist consciousness and action.[26]

---

[24] W. Oddie, *What will happen to God?* (London, SPCK, 1984); G. Leonard,
Let God be God (London, Darton, Longman and Todd, 1989). For an extended
discussion of the views of such opponents of Christian feminism, see M. Furlong,
A Dangerous Delight: Women and Power in the Church (London, SPCK, 1991),
Chapter 4.

[25] Figures such as Josephine Butler, Elizabeth Cady Stanton and Sojourner
Truth are all examples of those whose commitment to the rights of women was
inseparable from a devout faith.

[26] E.L. Graham and M. Halsey (eds.), *Life-Cycles: Women and Pastoral Care*
(SPCK, 1993).

First, it enabled the voices of women's experiences of pastoral care, and the diversity of their needs and contexts, to be heard. Second, it suggested that 'pastoral care' embraces more than personal counselling or support and that the process of giving and receiving care is about building relationships of mutuality and empowerment, of presence at the cutting edge of social change, of solidarity with the marginalized and of the provision of symbolic, ritual and theological resources by which people can make sense of their lives. By this token, critical and reconstructive practical theology starts with experience, attempts to place an individual story in a social or collective context, locates the personal story in relation to the stories of faith (both historical and contemporary) and finally encourages new models of practice to blossom which embody and enact renewed visions of faith. Such renewed practice may be, as contributors to the volume suggested, liturgical, or it may be embodied in new patterns of ministry, or expressed in 'breaking open' the fixed truths of Scripture and tradition. Fundamentally, such a transformation of *praxis* envisages a renewed feminist pastoral care to be 'word made flesh':[27]

> Christian pastoral practice has the potential to reveal a God who is startlingly present in human encounter. In their relationships and actions of care, Christians believe they can effect some of the creative and redemptive work of God, but that such care will also express something of the divine reality. Thus human pastoral relationships, however expressed, will also be to Christians in some sense a disclosure of God.[28]

I now turn to an illustration of one particular inclusive liturgical and reflection group, the St. Hilda Community, which represents some of the most profound and innovative theology in Britain today. It is significant, however, that this group is actually undertaking the *theological* task of critique and reconstruction from the vantage-point of *practical and pastoral* concern. It is therefore out

---

[27] Graham and Halsey (eds.), *Life-Cycles*, p. 234.
[28] E.L. Graham, 'The Sexual Politics of Pastoral Care' in Graham and Halsey (eds.), *Life-Cycles*, p. 220.

of specific pastoral responses to the complexities of women's experiences, that is, out of feminist *praxis*[29], that some of the most exciting feminist theology is emerging.

From exile to sanctuary: liturgy, community and theology

The origins of the St. Hilda Community lie in the exclusion and marginalization of women within the Church and the agonizing progress towards the ordination of women in the Church of England. It took nearly two decades, from the Church's General Synod declaring in 1975 there was 'no fundamental theological objection' to women priests, to the vote finally being passed in favour of women's ordination in November 1992. The first women were ordained priests in March 1994.[30]

These were wilderness years for many women and men in the Church of England. Their frustration and alienation was also shared to greater or lesser extent by other denominations. Traditions which did admit women to ordained ministry often afforded them less than equal standing and respect.[31] This general dissatisfaction coupled with the feeling (already noted) that the scope of feminist change was not exhausted by the single issue of ordination, encouraged activists to explore new avenues. One outcome was the establishment of informal worshipping communities concerned to promote women's ministry. They were not necessarily eucharistic, although on many occasions Non-Conformist women ministers or Anglican priests from overseas presided. The groups' intention was more to create liturgical and spiritual 'spaces' in which non-sexist and inclusive practice could be fostered. The St.

---

[29] I use the term *praxis* to mean value-informed and value-directed action, or 'truth as practicable', to paraphrase Jürgen Moltmann. The primacy of *praxis* as an arbiter of authentic theological understanding owes much to Liberation Theology. For a discussion of its relevance for feminist theology, see L. Hogan, *From Women's Experience to Feminist Theology* (Sheffield, Sheffield Academic Press, 1995).

[30] Dowell and Williams (eds.), *Bread, wine and women*, pp. 113-115.

[31] McEwan (ed.), *Women Experiencing Church*.

Hilda Community was one such, and serves as a good case-study because of the amount of attention it has received. Its story is recorded in a collection of liturgies and prayers, *Women Included.* Accompanying essays tell the story of the St. Hilda Community from its early beginnings in a college chapel in the East End of London.[32]

Many aspects of the St. Hilda experience mirror familiar contours of the 'Women-church' movement.[33] As well as this global referent, however, the St. Hilda Community, in common with many similar groups throughout Britain, also introduced elements of indigenous Christian tradition. The inspiration for the St. Hilda Community is the historical figure of Hilda of Whitby (614-80 CE), Abbess, teacher and theologian. As an influential supporter of Christian missions and scholarship, she occupies a prominent place in the history of the English church. As an example of a powerful woman in Christian antiquity, she has also been adopted as a proto-feminist icon by many women and men in the church. She therefore served as a highly suitable and inspirational 'patron saint' for a liturgical community concerned to retrieve and renew women's ministry in the church.[34]

The St. Hilda Community is also interesting in that it combined both pastoral and theological dimensions in its liturgical practice. It quite deliberately set out to be a place where the wounds of exclusion and sexism could be healed. Monica Furlong, a founder member, and Suzanne Fageol, a priest ordained in the United

---

[32] The St. Hilda Community, *Women included: A Book of Services and Prayers* (London, SPCK, 1991), Part One. The Community started meeting in 1987, was evicted from St. Benet's by the Diocese of London in 1989, moved to Methodist premises nearby and continued to meet right up to the first ordinations in 1994. Meetings are now held more informally in members' homes.

[33] See Rosemary Radford Ruether, *Women-Church: Theology and Practice* (San Francisco, Harper & Row, 1986). The 'women-church' movement, established in the United States and subsequently spreading throughout the world, is a network of alternative worship, liturgy and social action groups. Ruether's model is one of 'spirit-filled community' existing in critical parallel to the institutional Church.

[34] M. Furlong, 'A 'Non-Sexist' Community' in *Women Included: a Book of Services and Prayers* (London, SPCK, 1991), pp. 7-8.

States and occasional president, both comment on the powerful hurts and emotions which were frequently disclosed in the context of public worship.[35]

Thus, St. Hilda Community was always more than an experimental liturgical workshop: it was also genuinely an alternative community which provided a nurturing, supportive antidote to a patriarchal church. A deliberate policy was made whereby anyone attending a liturgy was considered to be part of the Community while they were visiting; and mutual care took precedence over set liturgies or formal proceedings: 'Nurturing and care-giving always take precedence over worship. If we cannot care for one another, how can we possibly hope to incarnate effectively the One in whose name we gather to worship?'[36] There was therefore an essential unity between hearing the stories of human hope and suffering, and enacting an alternative community which sought to transform current practice by prefiguring new ways of living.

From Women-church to God-talk

Whilst the St. Hilda Community is one of the better-known alternative liturgical groups, there are many such networks in varying degrees of organizational shape. Yet they represent an important focus for the devotional and spiritual lives of many who find the institutional churches restrictive or stifling. Circulating amongst these groups is an extensive array of liturgies, rites and prayers, some of which draws from established ecumenical sources such as the Community of Reconciliation at Taizé, the Iona Community, or the published work of contemporary writers

---

[35] Furlong, 'A 'Non-Sexist' Community'. S. Fageol, 'Celebrating Experience' in *Women Included: a Book of Services and Prayers* (London, SPCK, 1991), pp. 16-26. St. Hilda liturgies used dance, silence, symbolism as well as new forms of words; an emphasis on the creative use of space is also noteworthy (Fageol, p. 22).

[36] Fageol, 'Celebrating Experience', p. 21.

such as Janet Morley, Brian Wren and Jim Cotter.[37] Yet, in the best spirit of 'kitchen-table theology', such work probably represents the tip of an iceberg of *ad hoc*, unpublished creative writing distributed amongst and between such groups and communities. Much of this material which first came to birth in alternative worship groups has now filtered into mainstream congregations. It is therefore clear that one of the most significant legacies of such groups has been to force the question of inclusive language in worship onto the pastoral and liturgical agenda of the institutional churches.

Feminist theology is often accused by conservative commentators of being obsessed with so-called 'inclusive language'. It is argued that such a preoccupation with forms of words has nothing to do with theology (as a discourse of eternal truths) and reflects, once more, the extent to which feminist theologians are merely parroting the concerns of the 'politically correct' secular world. The complex matter of the relationship between human consciousness, cultural context and symbolic imagery[38] is thus reduced to the simplistic notion that feminist liturgists and theologians seek merely to swap all references to God as Father with those of God as Mother. Often these arguments are further bolstered by the accusation that Christian feminists are 'goddess worshippers'; another method of decrying the legitimacy of fem-

---

[37] J. Morley, *All Desires Known* (London, Movement for the Ordination of Women, 1988); B. Wren, *Bring Many Names* (Oxford, Oxford University Press, 1989; J. Cotter, *Prayer at Night: A Book for the Darkness* (Sheffield, Cairns Publications, 1988). For representative samples of the best of such recent work, see H. Ward, J. Wild and J. Morley (eds.), *Celebrating Women*, 2nd edn (London, SPCK, 1995) and H. Ward and J. Wild (eds.), *Human Rites: Worship Resources for an Age of Change* (London, Mowbray, 1995).

[38] The work of Sallie McFague provides a well-argued and provocative exposition of the philosophical underpinnings of religious language. She argues for a clear link between images of the sacred and divine and patterns of social relations. Language is necessarily shaped by cultural and political context, but must always be seen as provisional and contingent: a 'Model' not an 'Idol'. See *Metaphorical Theology: Models of God in Religious Language* (London, SCM, 1983); and *Models of God: Theology for an Ecological Nuclear Age* (London, SCM, 1987).

inist claims, of course, by placing them 'beyond the pale' of orthodox belief.[39]

The reality is far more nuanced, and more profound. It is not a question of mere forms of words but relates to theological questions about who God is for us. Language about God is crucial to our experiences of God, and to our spirituality, because language does not simply reflect, but also actively shapes, human consciousness.[40] Inclusive language is one means of enabling worshippers to envision new models of divine agency. Inclusive imagery for the worshipping community also helps women to feel visible as full participants in the Body of Christ.[41]

> As Christian women we need to celebrate our creativity, on all levels. We are called to open the church, and men, as well as ourselves, to the idea that we are originally blessed in the image of God and as connected to the rest of creation … St. Hilda's members have constructed whole liturgies around the celebration of God as our Mother, as the one who gives birth to and nurtures us into creative adulthood. The Hebrew bible is a rich source for such wisdom and celebration. There we find images of God as Holy Wisdom who teaches us spiritual discernment and God as 'ruach', the feminine wind-energy who brings creation out of chaos.[42]

Clearly, what I have already said about a Christian community 'incarnating' and embodying its truth-claims in its collective practice is fundamental to the self-understanding of the St. Hilda Community. This is apparent in the way the community resolved the dilemma of appropriate leadership and presidency. Faced with the

---

[39] See Oddie, *What will happen to God?* and Leonard, *Let God be God.* For a reasoned defence of inclusive language, see D. Carmody, *Responses to 101 Questions about Feminism* (London, Geoffrey Chapman, 1994).

[40] See McFague, *Metaphorical Theology.*

[41] Liturgical Commission, General Synod of the Church of England, *Making Women Visible* (London, Church House Publishing, 1989). Note that this report welcomes cautiously the idea of inclusive language for congregations but refuses to be drawn into debates about language for God. For further discussion on the inclusive language debate, see J. Morley, "The Faltering Words of Men': Exclusive Language in the Liturgy' in M. Furlong (ed.), *Feminine in the Church* (London, SPCK, 1984), pp. 56-70.

[42] Fageol, 'Celebrating Experience', p. 24.

non-availability of women's priestly ministry (legally at least), and a preference not to have male presidents at its liturgies, the St. Hilda Community had to search for new models. It was decided to undertake a collective adoption of actions normally restricted to the priest: absolution, eucharist and blessing. In the corporate actions which developed as a result, mere expediency was transformed into a powerful symbolic expression of shared ministry and community:

> Mutual absolution takes the form of a shared general confession, drawn from various sources, feminist and other... This sacramental act, normally preserved as the priest's, is powerful when done personally and as a shared ministry of the whole body of Christ. The depth of forgiveness, given and received, brings us all closer to God and to each other as images of God incarnate.[43]

Insofar as the St. Hilda liturgies occupy a perilous space between critique and reconstruction, there will always be a tension between the old and the new. Finding a comfortable resting-place in an androcentric tradition is not easy, and feminist theology is beset with choices about the extent to which the historical tradition can be retrieved as 'usable' and 'woman-friendly', or else abandoned completely as corrupt and irredeemable.[44] One strategy of reconstruction is to recover formerly hidden voices and testimonies from the past and consciously to celebrate them. The lives and examples of Hilda of Whitby and Julian of Norwich have been valorized by Christian feminists in Britain and beyond in just such a fashion. But is this alternative 'herstory' ever quite so rich and unproblematic as the malestream history? It is, after all, a heritage of scraps and fragments: and whilst feminist theologians may pride themselves on their enterprise of 'searching for lost coins'[45]

---

[43] Fageol, Celebrating Experience', p. 20.

[44] Such choices inform much of the debate in D. Hampson (ed.), *Swallowing a Fishbone?* and formed the central issue in the dialogue between Hampson and Ruether. See D. Hampson and R.R. Ruether, 'Is there a Place for Feminists in a Christian Church?' *New Blackfriars*, (January 1987), 7-24.

[45] A. Loades, *Searching for Lost Coins: Explorations in Christianity and Feminism* (London, SPCK, 1987).

this arguably still only amounts to the gathering of the small change of Christian history. Feminist practical theologians are compelled to assert that 'tradition' is never a final and absolute authority for contemporary *praxis*. It is clear from the examples discussed earlier that the voices and contexts of the present, reflecting the changes, complexities and contradictions of 'women's experience', have the right to challenge the fixity and authority of the past. In the meeting of horizons between past and present, heritage and experience, the practical, concrete and immediate demands of gender justice calls forth new theological insights; an admission that the tradition as it stands is not adequate.

This is clearly illustrated with reference to the St. Hilda Community, where many of the liturgies and prayers have deliberately rewritten traditional forms in a conscious reappropriation. Some of the most well-known – and widely-used – feminist prayers are Janet Morley's 'Collects' (designated prayers for the day in the Anglican tradition). They rehearse the themes and cadences of traditional forms but deploy startling new imagery:

> God our mother,
> you hold our life within you;
> nourish us at your breast,
> and teach us to walk alone.
> Help us so to receive your tenderness
> and respond to your challenge
> that others may draw life from us,
> in your name. Amen.[46]

The St. Hilda Community is one example of how women's naming of their experiences, their purposeful enactment of caring practice and their conscious attempts to reclaim the sacred are actively contributing to a recreation of Christian tradition in theory *and* practice. Although the Community was always open to women and men, it also had a special vocation by which it '... existed to give space to women'.[47] This metaphor of space is one to which I

[46] St. Hilda Community, *Women Included*, p. 45.
[47] Fageol, 'Celebrating Experience', p. 18.

find myself returning.[48] It is a powerful idea by which to explore many creative avenues in feminist theology: to what extent is all pastoral practice, be it counselling, preaching, listening, telling stories, times of meditation or worship, essentially about creating the space in which human and divine encounters can flourish?

Underpinning and articulating feminist models of care, community and worship are renewed visions of the Divine; and it is here that we can see how new theological responses are being forged. I detect clear parameters of a novel and exciting feminist practical theology in which there is no separation between Christian practice and 'God-talk' because each feeds and stimulates the other. Incongruously perhaps, practical theologians are wont to quote the Church of England Alternative Service Book to illustrate this point: 'Christians are formed by the way in which they pray, and the way they choose to pray expresses what they are'[49]; but for me, this is an excellent example of feminist pastoral *praxis* in which reflection and action, word and deed, are fused into a life-giving theology. Feminist liturgical communities like the St. Hilda Community are therefore essentially doxological, shaped by their purposeful encounters with the divine in worship, and defined by an attempt to embody and enact their theology in their collective practice, as forms of 'words made flesh'.

Conclusion: new horizons

In the midst of emergent voices within practical theology a feminist perspective is galvanizing the discipline and pointing to new challenges for the future. I wish finally to identify three crucial priorities for feminist practical theology in Britain: dialogue with the discipline as a whole, dialogue across ethnic and racial boundaries and dialogue with 'secular' feminists.

[48] See E.L. Graham, 'From 'Space' to 'Woman-Space'', *Feminist Theology*, 9 (May 1995), 11-34.
[49] *The Alternative Service Book* (Oxford, Mowbray, 1980), p. 10; Furlong, 'A 'Non-Sexist' Community', p. 5.

Issues of social inequality continue to occupy practical theologians, reinforcing work which has already argued for a clearer commitment to 'the politics of pastoral care'.[50] Significantly, Stephen Pattison in a recent work on the relationship between liberation theology and pastoral care has identified gender issues, and more specifically women's lack of status and power in relation to mental health, as a major priority for pastors, health care chaplains and policy-makers.[51]

Whilst feminist theology and gender issues may be making some impact on academic practical theology, however, Christian feminist theology still faces challenges of its own. There is much to be done to address issues of religious pluralism and racial injustice, although gradually, the voices of Black Christian women are breaking through. The experience of exclusion from many white-majority denominations in the years following mass immigration from the West Indies after 1945, has been decisive in forging Black British Christians' self-understanding and is similar to the collective memory of slavery for African-Americans. Women in Black-majority churches are beginning to tell their stories: naming experience, resisting exclusion and remaking the tradition in their own ways.[52]

A final question concerns how a Christian feminist practical theology might respond to the spiritual needs of women who have left the churches or choose to channel their energies into other forms of spirituality. Can suitable spaces – studies, kitchens, sanctuaries, churches, pulpits – be created in which fruitful dialogue can take place? How will Christian feminists break down the barriers of suspicion and indifference on the part of 'secular' feminists? These are all critical tests of the ultimate reality and relevance of a feminist practical theology, in its ability to offer anything of worth to a society beyond the Christian walls.

[50] P. Selby, *Liberating God: Private Care and Public Struggle* (London, SPCK, 1983).

[51] S. Pattison, *Pastoral Care and Liberation Theology* (Cambridge, Cambridge University Press, 1994).

[52] E. Pitts, 'Black Womanist Ethic' in P. Grant and R. Patel (eds.), *A Time to Speak: Perspectives of Black Christians in Britain* (Birmingham, Community and Race Relations Unit, 1990), pp. 29-35.

Feminist theory may offer some important clues as to the future direction of feminist practical theology. I have identified a number of locations and contexts for such theological action and reflection: academy, kitchen and sanctuary. All are an essential part of the vitality of contemporary feminist practical theology, witnessing to the fact that we cannot separate theory from practice, the esoteric from the everyday, intellectual discovery from social responsibility. These various contexts speak well of our experiences as women in modern Britain; but does such diversity militate against coherence? Significantly, contemporary feminist theory argues that pluralism and difference are a necessary part of our thinking and acting. To assume one dominant story or framework is to risk marginalizing and silencing those whose experiences do not correspond with the 'master narrative'. Yet the alternative is not to collapse into relativism or the babel of competing voices. As Donna Haraway argues, we can recognize that the voices of difference represent 'situated knowledges', all of which reflect legitimate vantage-points.[53] To be clear about the space from which we speak and act is, for Haraway, a guarantee of an ethically responsible perspective on truth:

> Feminists don't need a doctrine of objectivity that promises transcendence, a story that loses track of its mediations just where someone might be held responsible for something, and unlimited instrumental power. We don't want a theory of innocent powers to represent the world, where language and bodies fall into the bliss of organic symbiosis. We also don't want to theorize the world, much less act within it, in terms of Global Systems, but we do need an earthwide network of connections, including the ability partially to translate knowledges among very different – and power-differentiated – communities. We need the power of modern critical theories of how meanings and bodies get made, not in order to deny meanings and bodies, but in order to build meanings and bodies that have a chance for life.[54]

I take heart, therefore, from the understanding that feminist practical theologies, born of pastoral practice, directed towards specific

[53] D. Haraway, *Cyborgs, Simians and Women* (London, Polity Press, 1991), pp. 187-196.

[54] Haraway, *Cyborgs, Simians and Women*, p. 187.

aims and ends of care, nurture and celebration, can claim to be 'situated knowledges' about justice, love and the divine.

It is hard to negotiate some of the differences, and the competing loyalties which often arise, let alone gain recognition from institutions which frequently attempt to constrain or categorize us within their domains. Feminist practical theologians, whether they work in the academy, the church, at home, or in the political world, need to be mutually accountable and supportively critical. In Manchester, we try to embody these different contexts and perspectives, and to engage with one another in collaborative *praxis* in teaching and learning together; and I hope that, like the cherry tree, our work is the sign of a blossoming forth of vital and vibrant new life.

ADDITIONAL BIBLIOGRAPHY

Alexander, Valentina. "'A Mouse in a Jungle': the Black Christian Women's Experience in the Church and Society in Britain' in Delia Jarrett Macauley (ed.), *Reconstructing Womanhood, Reconstructing Feminism*, London, Routledge, 1996, pp. 85-108

Durber, Susan and Walton, Heather (eds.), *Silence in Heaven: a book of women's preaching*, London, SCM, 1994

Graham, Elaine L. *Transforming Practice: Pastoral Theology in an Age of Uncertainty*, London, Mowbray, 1996

Maitland, Sara. *A Map of the New Country: Women and Christianity*, London, Routledge and Kegan Paul, 1993

Ortega, Ofelia (ed.), *Women's Visions: Theological Reflection, Celebration, Action*, Geneva, WCC Publications, 1995

Stuart, Elizabeth (ed.), *Daring to Speak Love's Name: a Gay and Lesbian Prayer Book*, London, Hamish Hamilton, 1992

Webster, Alison (ed.), *Found Wanting: Women, Christianity and Sexualty*, London, Cassell, 1995

VIII

Genetic testing:
the tree of the knowledge of good
and evil

Barbara NICHOLAS

> And the Lord God commanded... saying,
> 'You may eat of every tree in the garden;
> but of the tree of the knowledge of good
> and evil you shall not eat, for in the day
> that you eat of it you shall die...' So
> when the woman saw that the tree was
> good for food, and that it was a delight
> to the eyes, and that the tree was to be
> desired to make one wise, she took of the
> fruit and ate ... To the woman God said,
> 'I will greatly multiply your pain in child-
> bearing; in pain you shall bring forth
> children, yet your desire shall be for your
> husband and he shall rule over you.'

Introduction

Since the writing of the creation story, reflections on women
and God have frequently focussed on conception and childbirth,
and their significance in giving identity and status to women.
In this paper I will use a contemporary feature of childbearing in
the developed world, namely, pre-natal genetic screening, as a
focus for reflection on the nature and practice of feminist practical
theology.

The context

New Zealand is a country in the midst of massive social change and debate. Over the last fifteen years or so there has been a significant move to the political right. An ideology of free trade and the 'delights' of market forces have come to dominate our political landscape. Accompanying these emerging changes in government policy has come reduced international debt, claims of wealth creation, a reduction in the commitment to a welfare state, an increased gap between rich and poor and fluctuating but high unemployment. Recent changes[1] in the method of electing parliament have added to a powerful sense of political movement and transition.

In addition to the move to the right, *other political forces* have also been operating. The feminist movement, particularly in the 1970s and 1980s, made some significant gains for women. It has also been a period of negotiation for a changing relationship between the indigenous people (Maori) and the dominant culture (pakeha). Maori are claiming their rightful political power, resisting assimilation and continuing colonisation. They are reminding the rest of the nation that we can not successfully move forward without addressing the abuses of Maori people and the confiscation of their lands.

New Zealand is also a developed country, with all the accompanying expectations of lifestyle and access to resources and technology. We expect the benefits of science, technology and medicine to be available to us all. Our academic institutions are part of the world-wide networks of funding, scholarship and people taken for granted by the developed world. But we are also discovering the attendant complications and dilemmas. For instance, despite their many benefits, science and technology are confronting us with funding choices, the availability of such funding, and through which political and social processes it will take place. How will we deal with all the possibilities inherent in New Reproductive Technologies, genetic manipulation and expensive medical treatment?

---

[1] Until 1996, members of Parliament (MPs) all represented electorates, and were elected on the basis of one person – one vote. Recent changes give all voters two votes – one for an electorate representative and one for a party.

The tensions and debates about which direction the country should go are largely re-produced within the churches, whose membership reflects the diversity of the non-church-going population. Right wing Christian parties have emerged, valuing the family and promoting policies which give more support to married couples with children than to single parents or those in *de facto* relationships. But the churches are also involved in the food banks, and their social services pick up many of the casualities of economic reform. Some of the most critical comment on government policies is emerging from church bodies.

Feminist theology has been an important social and theological movement within New Zealand churches. Individual denominations have had distinct histories with regard to women in leadership, and at times the struggle for the ordination of women has dominated the political agenda of particular groups. But we are a small country, and reasonably mobile within it. Extensive networking has been a feature of feminist theology. There have been several national Feminist Conferences as well as local gatherings, various newsletters, and a continuing exchange of ideas, information and resources. Conferences have addressed issues of feminist spirituality, racism, poverty, Christology and the implications of doing theology in the Pacific.

There has been the space and freedom to explore a wide range of ideas, and, in terms of structural changes, the position of women in the Protestant churches has greatly improved over the last twenty years. Women in the Catholic Church have had a different experience; there has been and continues to be strong leadership from lay and religious women, but the church institution continues to marginalise most women from positions of leadership, and to resist initiatives for social and political change.

However, the integration of women into positions of leadership in the Protestant churches, at local and at national level, has not helped to resolve many theological issues. What it has shown is that having women leaders does not necessarily lead to any fundamental changes in theology and church practice. Some women within the church struggle to maintain a sense that things can be different. Other women decide that the continuing struggle within the churches to challenge assumptions of power, understandings of God, forms of liturgy and political involvement is no longer worth it, or that the christian faith is incompatible with what they hold most important.

My personal involvement in theology and bioethics is a product of this context. Few of my generation (born in the 1950s) have been able to form an adult faith separate from the political and social climate. Feminist debate, the South African Springbok rugby tour of 1981 (which politicised the entire country as we argued about whether or not politics should, or could, be kept separate from sport), the movements for social justice by the Maori, and protest about nuclear testing in the Pacific, were all important features of New Zealand life. The churches have struggled to find a way to respond to these issues, but it is notable that few of my generation have found a faith that keeps them within church structures.

I stayed immersed in the church for many years, and was even ordained an anglican priest. But all through that period I was concerned that theological thought and church practice, fascinating and stimulating though it was, failed to engage with the issues that faced the wider society. We were and are a society that is coping with change on many fronts, and I was struggling to find a way to understand and live with those changes. When the church did comment it often appeared to be from outside, protecting itself from questioning how theology and the institutional church functioned to sustain or transform what was happening in people's lives.

Coming to theology (rather than church practice) in order to think through the implications of my new found feminist analysis and commitments, I found that the method of liberation theology made sense to me. My working assumption was that theology should function to liberate and heal, and if it did not do that, then it was not good theology but merely a discourse that supported the power structures of the privileged. Liberation theology attracted me because it started with a description and questioning of the lived experiences of people's lives. How do people actually live? What constructs the possibilities for their lives? It also assumed that the experience of the most marginalised people mattered. In addition, liberation theology asked questions such as: 'how does this myth, or doctrine, or language, function to sustain or transform those possibilities?' It was not an application *to the world* of church doctrine or of traditional theological insights, but a more interactive process that allowed lived experience to question the adequacy or otherwise of theology, however that theology might presently be articulated.

I now work in a Bioethics Research Centre, located in a medical school, in a department that offers graduate programmes in health ethics and an undergraduate programme which students may include in their science, arts or theology degrees. Here I am involved, amongst other things, in discussions about changing technologies and medical developments that are dramatically changing women's experiences.

Feminist practical theology

My understanding of *practical* theology has been shaped by this history and context. Practical theology needs, first of all, to be related to the experience of people's lives, since my fundamental assumption is that theology and spirituality should function to liberate and heal real people in actual situations. Practical theology needs to be about how people live, and the social and political conditions that form the choices open to them. Practical theology is context-specific. It does not try to subsume the particulars of people's lives into universal truths, but embraces the specifics of different lives as the grounding for the work of an ongoing reflection and action, based in the conviction that God-talk matters.

Secondly, practical theology is about the different interpretive frameworks through which people make meaning of their lives. It questions how interpretive frameworks function. Do they serve to reinforce and reproduce oppressive social relationships? Or do they function to undermine, destabilise and transform those same relationships? Interpretive frameworks are never neutral. They act as filters through which we pass our experiences in order to make sense of them. Thus different filters or interpretive frameworks will give weighting and significance to different things in different ways.[2]

This second aspect of practical theology reflects my assumption that good theology is transformative and liberating. It is possible to see practical theology as only theological reflection on lived experience. In this case one would be trying to make sense of the realities of people's lives within traditional frameworks of understanding and meaning. I would argue that good practical theology cannot stop at that point, but as a theology committed to transformation and healing on every level, practical theology must also include engagement with the very interpretive frameworks which structure and constrain the possibilities we can imagine. How does any theological approach function (socially, politically, ideologically) for particular groups of people in particular contexts?

I see *feminist* practical theology as one subset of practical theology. It has a particular focus – on women's lives, the varieties of their lived experiences, and the particular features of their lives that are structured or constrained by a sexist society and theology.

In the feminist theology that has emerged over that last thirty years or so we can find illustrations of the way in which practical theology can function to liberate at both the level of immediate experience, and at the level of the theology or framework for interpretation. The 'normal', accepted, or commonsensical ways of organising and maintaining social relationships have been questioned and reviewed, and the possibilities for women changed. For example, at one time it was obvious that only men could be

---

[2] For instance, my understanding of mothering is affected by a number of different interpretive frameworks. Some are cultural. I am a middle-class, educated woman, daughter of traditional middle-class English parents. It did not really occur to me to put my children in day-care. I assumed that I should be the primary carer, all the time. My interpretation of my role was reinforced by the particular Christian tradition in which I lived, with its ideology of the family reinforced by particular representations of the Christian family, Jesus's family and the family of God. Traditional understandings of the role of women did nothing to question my assumptions.

ordained, and that women were called to particular ministries such as hospitality, church cleaning and child care. Feminist practical theology has wondered if and why that need be so. We began to imagine what it might be like for the world to be different, and for women to celebrate Eucharist. To even imagine that possibility was to begin to change the world!

As feminists began to imagine a different world on a social and institutional level, traditional articulations of theology also began to be transformed. If women as well as men are made in God's image, then maybe we can talk about God as female as well as male. And as we questioned whether relationships of domination and submission between husband and wife were healthy or appropriate, we began to identify ways in which theology is riddled with patriarchal assumptions that say more about the people who transmit and interpret the tradition[3] than about the nature of God.

In my work in bioethics I find myself continually moving between these two foci – the lived experience of women, and the framework through which women can analyse their experience and make decisions about the possibilities that face them.

In the remainder of this paper I want to look at the implications for women, and for practical feminist theology, of pre-conception and pre-natal genetic testing. This is an expression of *feminist practical* theology because I am starting with an aspect of women's lives. I am exploring how the interpretive frameworks of our theology or culture help women to understand the situations they are in, and to make meaning. I am inquiring how our talk of God contributes to the possibilities of healing and liberation (or continues to oppress).

Genetic knowledge and the possibilities for choice

Science and medicine are offering women possibilities for choice that were hardly envisaged even a decade ago. It is not just

---

[3] I am using the term 'tradition' in a very lose sense, as a general term to encompass our biblical, theological and historical Christian heritage.

a choice whether or not to have children, but a choice about what sort of children we will have – and about living with responsibilities that are being thrust upon us, whether we want them or not[4].

Genetic information is passed from parents to children. Each of us receives a copy of each parent's genes. Some genes are dominant, that is, if the individual carries a dominant gene it will express itself, regardless of the matching gene inherited from the other parent. Other genes are recessive, that is, they will only express themselves if there are two copies present, one inherited from each parent. However, although the recessive gene may not express itself in the individual, the individual is able to pass that gene on to any children. Depending on the child's other parent's contribution, the gene may then express itself in the next generation.[5]

Some genetic conditions, such as cystic fibrosis[6] and Huntington's[7], are caused by changes in only one gene. Other genetic con-

---

[4] This is a technology that is more likely to be offered to women in the developed world, and this is the context in which I live. However, the potential of any technology to further perpetuate and even extend present patterns of oppression and exploitation is illustrated by another screening technology, ultra-sound, which has managed to find its way into the lives of women in the developing world. In India, for example, it is widely available even in areas where basic health care is extremely limited. Here its most frequent use is to detect the sex of the foetus, and 'assist' women to make the decision to selectively abort female foetuses. See Kusum, 'The use of prenatal diagnosis for sex selection: the Indian scene', *Bioethics* 7:2/3 (1993), 149-165.

[5] The exception to the general rule that recessive genes need to be present from both parents is sex-linked conditions. Here if the gene is on the X chromosome (which is from the mother), and there is no matching gene on the Y-chromosome (which is from the father), a male may express the recessive gene. A female may carry the gene but will not express it unless she also inherits the same form of the gene from her father. Some sex-linked genetic conditions, such as muscular dystrophy, have this basis.

[6] Cystic fibrosis is a recessive disease of the exocrine glands (those that produce sweat, saliva and digestive juices). Thick tacky secretions tend to block airways, leading to frequent severe chest infections with prolonged and severe coughing. Children used to die before puberty, but life expectancy has extended considerably with better treatment options.

[7] Huntington's is a dominantly inherited condition, characterised by choreic movements and progressive mental retardation, leading to death. There is a variable age of onset, but generally symptoms appear in a person's forties, after she/he has made reproductive decisions and may already have children.

ditions are more complex and involve a number of genes. The presence of a particular gene may not, in itself, determine that a genetic condition will develop – it may just make it more likely. For example, there is some evidence of a genetic basis for the early onset of heart disease, but whether or not the heart disease develops will also be influenced by environmental factors such as diet and exercise.

Our understandings of genetics is increasing rapidly, particularly since the establishment of the Human Genome Project which is seeking to map the entire human genotype. This project offers the possibility of understanding the genetic component of many conditions, and the hope of new possibilities for treatment and choice. However, it is important to note that the conditions or expressions now being looked at are not only 'medical conditions', but issues such as whether there is a genetic basis for homosexuality or criminal behaviour.

Implications of reproductive choices

This expanding genetic knowledge is offering new choices of treatment and care to people with a number of different conditions. But the area which has experienced the greatest impact from this knowledge, and its associated technology, is reproduction. Whereas up to about twenty years ago a woman had no choice about the sort of child she would bear, the ability to test for the presence of certain genes now presents her with choices at a number of stages.

There are three stages in reproductive decision-making when women may be presented with choices as a result of technologies of genetic testing – before conception, at conception and once pregnant.

For those who know of a family history of a genetic condition there is an increasing likelihood that they will be offered a test to establish whether or not they carry that gene. More and more accurate information is available to women to let them know the level of risk associated with their choices, and assist them to make decisions about whether or not to begin a pregnancy.[8]

In-vitro fertilisation (fertilisation of an egg in a 'test tube' with subsequent implantation in the woman's womb) presents another possible occasion to use genetic tests. Once embryos have been fertilised, and prior to them being introduced into a woman's body, it is possible to test for the presence of suspected genes. It is usual for there to be more than one embryo available, and, it can be argued, it is only sensible to implant the embryo that will have the best chance of leading to a healthy child. A woman unable to choose an abortion, yet wanting to ensure that a gene is not passed on, could choose to conceive using in vitro fertilisation.[9]

Genetic testing can also be carried out after conception, within the first weeks of gestation.[10] This is likely to become the most

[8] In recent decades some genetic counselling has been possible which has informed people of the probability of carrying a gene, based on the taking of a family history. For example, if a woman's brother expressed the condition of muscular dystrophy (a sex linked condition, inherited from the mother who does not herself express it), then there is a 50% chance that she will carry that gene. If so, she will transmit it to sons (who will express the disease), and her own daughters will have a 50% chance of inheriting the gene from her, and passing it on to their sons. If the gene was expressed in more distant relatives then a more extensive family history would be taken, and probabilities might be established in a more indirect way. But they would only be probabilities – only through having a child would one know if the gene had been passed on.

With the establishment of molecular genetic tests, probabilities could be established more precisely. This did/does require the taking of body samples from family members, and some comparison of DNA profiles. The more family members available to give samples, the more accurate the information.

Now an increasing number of tests are being developed where samples from family members are not required, but the presence or absence of the gene for a particular condition can be established to a fairly high level of accuracy from just one person's body tissue.

[9] This technology has now been used by a family to select for female embryos. The 'parents had selected girls because severe genetic disease had affected three previous pregnancies with male embryos.' (*Otago Daily Times*, June 22, 1996.)

[10] There are two techniques that can be used – amniocentesis and chorionic villi sampling. Amniocentesis takes place at sixteen to twenty weeks' gestation and involves the insertion of a hollow needle through the woman's abdomen and into the amniotic sac. A small sample of amniotic fluid (which contains foetal cells) is removed, allowed to divide in the laboratory, and then analysed. Chronic villi sampling is the more recent technique, which can be carried out at ten to

common time that genetic testing is available to women. Indeed some forms are almost routine in some countries. For example, in New Zealand it is quite usual for women over thirty five to be offered amniocentesis to check for Down's Syndrome, a condition that becomes more frequent with increasing maternal age. Amniocentesis may also be offered to women with a known family history of some conditions.[11]

The *availability* of prenatal testing presents women with two choices. Firstly, there is the choice of whether or not to have genetic tests in the first place. Some women are sure that the results of the test will make no difference to their decisions about proceeding with the pregnancy, and hence do not have the test at all; they do not want the information. If one chooses to go ahead with genetic tests, there is a further choice: which tests to have. As genetic knowledge continues to expand and more tests become available, the range of options will also expand. Some tests are for life threatening conditions in early infancy; others for life threatening conditions that express themselves later in life. Some tests are for conditions that will definitely express themselves if the gene is present; others for genes that increase the chances of a condition. For some genetic conditions therapy is available; for others, changes in their lifestyle after their birth, may reduce the risk and improve the prognosis. There is also the chance that a therapy may be available by the time a child needs it. There are wider considerations as well. In addition to any questions about abortion (which I am not addressing in this discussion) there are all the possibilities of genetic information being used against one in insurance and employment, or of a subtle eugenics to discrimi-

---

eleven weeks' gestation and thus provides information much earlier in the pregnancy. There is some debate about the safety of this procedure for the developing foetus. (See Jane A. Evans and John L. Hamerton, 'Limb defects and chorionic villi sampling', *Lancet*, 347:(9000) (1996), 489.) This procedure involves insertion of a catheter through the vagina and cervix and the extraction, for testing, of cells from the placenta.

[11] See Adrienne Ash and Gail Geller, 'Feminism, bioethics and genetics' in S.M. Wolf (ed.), *Feminism and Bioethics: Beyond Reproduction* (Oxford, New York, Oxford University Press, 1996).

nate against those who differ from dominant conceptions of 'normal'.

There are many grey areas where the benefits of genetic knowledge are not obvious, such as knowing that one carries the gene for early onset of Alzheimer's disease.

Once a person has had tests, there is a second choice – how to respond to the information gained. Sometimes the information gained is reassuring (the possible gene is not there), other times one discovers or confirms the presence of a harmful gene, and a woman may be presented with the choice of continuing or terminating a pregnancy.

This choice, like so many which women must make, may be quite complicated. The tests are usually carried out for a pregnancy that the woman is planning or hoping to carry to term. If a harmful gene has been discovered, one has to make a judgement about the appropriateness of continuing with the pregnancy. Yet families who have cared for children born with Tay-Sachs[12], or who have watched family members struggle with cystic fibrosis, or die from Huntington's, know that such judgements are not simple. That person's life has been one of pain and distress, and however much their family may have loved them, there is little wish to have more children with the condition.

A family or a woman may also be counting the cost of care for a child requiring intensive care. However much one may hope for the sort of supportive community where the care of the sick or handicapped is shared, frequently the reality is that the burden of care falls on a few, often women. Those with a disability also need to contend with continuing discrimination. Like all choices about reproduction, choice about responses to genetic testing is made in a total life context. Women are situated in a web of relationships and commitments. Decisions are made with attention to other responsibilities, and mindful of the context in which one lives.

---

[12] Tay-sachs is a recessively inherited, degenerative neurological condition, causing severe mental and physical retardation and eventually death, usually by the age of four.

Choice and responsibility

Women also make these decisions within the imaginative and conceptual frameworks that are important to them. Once the options and facts are available to them, women must still weigh up the various possibilities, and choose a response. Those who live within the christian tradition will be affected by the attitudes to women, and to their responsibilities in childbearing, that are embedded within that heritage.

On one level, childbearing is valued. For instance, images of Madonna and child are frequent; each Christmas we extol the virtues of Mary and her embrace of motherhood. Motherhood is held out as the true vocation of women. But a number of feminist writers have pointed out the misogynist assumptions that underlie much of this promotion of motherhood, and the extent to which it is assumed that women, their sexuality, and their reproductive abilities must be controlled by men.[13] Women are rarely seen as moral agents, capable of making choices and bearing responsibility.

As women, we are realising the extent to which our understandings of ourselves, and of the limits of our responsibility, have been moulded by centuries of patriarchal religious tradition that understood our reproductive capacities in particular terms. It is a tradition that has painted the woman as the one who chose to take the fruit, whose fault it was that we were cast out of the garden of Eden, and the one for whom the pain and travail associated with childbirth is the consequence of choosing to eat of the tree of knowledge of good and evil.[14]

[13] See Karen Armstrong, *The Gospel According to Women* (London, Pan Books Ltd, 1987); Riet Bons-Storm, *The Incredible Woman* (Abingdon, Nashville Tn, 1996); Anne Carr and Elisabeth Schüssler Fiorenza, (eds.), *Motherhood: Experience, Institution, Theology, Concilium; Religion in the Eighties* (Edinburgh, T&T Clark, 1989); Elizabeth Schüssler Fiorenza, *In Memory of Her* (London, SCM Press, 1983); B. Harrison, *Our Right to Choose: Toward a New Ethics of Abortion* (Boston, Beacon, 1983); Rosemary Radford Ruether, *Sexism and God-talk* (London, SCM Press, 1983).

[14] See Elaine Pagels, *Adam, Eve, and the Serpent* (New York, Vintage Books, 1988); Ruether, *Sexism and God-talk*.

At the same time, the younger generation of women, those of childbearing years who live in the developed world, are being presented with the responsibility of deciding how they will use or respond to a new technology, available to 'assist' them in reproduction. They are being presented with possibilities that their foremothers never faced, and are being asked to make choices that are quite distinctive from other reproductive decisions. The decision is not whether or not to have a child, but whether or not to have this particular child, with her or his specific genetic heritage.

Be it unto me according to your word

It is possible to respond to all this in a very decisive way – to reject the technology, and to argue that it is totally unacceptable to select a child on the basis of its genetic heritage. One must love and accept, unquestionably, whatever God gives. Life is sacred. To intervene, to make judgements about which life to bring to birth is to move outside the bounds of 'acceptable' control of creation.

This is the simple solution – one which removes the dilemma. It is also an argument that relies heavily on a model of God as the (patriarchal) authority figure whom one must obey and to whom one must submit, without debate. God knows best. Mary, mother of Jesus, is the model here – a woman who does not question the action of God, but nurtures and cares for that which God brings. Mary has, through the centuries, been offered as the paradigm example of the good woman, the loving mother – totally obedient and submissive, all-giving. There is little place here for choice, little room for explorations, or for difficult questions. There is little sense that women are moral agents, called to live with all the responsibilities of human freedom. Obedience is all.

Mary, the good woman, is in sharp contrast to Eve. Centuries of interpretation of the second Genesis creation story have presented the disobedience of a woman as the reason for the expulsion of humanity from the garden of Eden, for their loss of innocence, and the subsequent need for the travail of women in childbirth and the toil of men in the earth. Eve's expression of choice is seen in terms of sin and blame, and the need for forgiveness and redemption.[15] The fall, the loss of the protection by creation, is woman's fault. It is the result of lack of obedience, lack of recognition of the limits established by God. Few interpretations of this story understand women's choice as a choice for responsibility, a move into mature relationship with God, an embracing of freedom.

This history of interpretation has had a direct impact on understandings of women's reproductive role. Women have not been encouraged to see themselves as moral agents. Expressing choice and accepting responsibility is not a virtue. Within a patriarchal tradition it is more likely to be seen as disobedience and rebellion.[16] Women have not been encouraged to exercise control over their reproductive capabilities, even while these reproductive capabilities have been used to define their social role. Nor have women been encouraged to protest or question an understanding of God as one who punishes those who express moral agency, and who does so through the experience of birth.

Yet, there is no justice in blaming a woman, or her family, for the suffering of a genetic condition. To talk of sin and forgiveness, repentance or obedience, is to burden women with guilt for a choice they must make in a situation that is not of their making. It makes no sense to see the burden of care of a family member, or the mental deterioration of a child, or the early onset of

[15] Interpretations of the creation story tend to fit Eve and the expression of freedom/responsibility into the paradigm of sin and (the need of) redemption. See for example Walter Brueggmann, 'Genesis' in J. L. Mays (ed.), *Interpretation: a Bible Commentary for Teaching and Preaching* (Atlanta, John Knox Press, 1982) who, in discussing the issue of the freedom of human persons assumes a context of prohibition by God. He argues that the genesis story moves from one of trust and obedience to one of crime and punishment. Such an interpretation sees choice as an expression of rebellion, not of responsibility.

[16] See Danna Nolan Fewell, 'Reading the Bible Ideologically: feminist criticism' in S. L. Mckenzie and S. R. Haynes (eds.), *To Each its Own Meaning: an Introduction to Biblical Criticisms and their Application* (Louisville, Kentucky, Westminster/John Knox Press, 1993); Newsom C. Trible and Sharon H. Ringe (eds.), *The Women's Bible Commentary* (London, SPCK, 1992).

Alzheimer's, or the knowledge that one is very likely to die of breast cancer, as a punishment for God knows what. We need to let go an understanding of God that relies on a judgemental, demanding father figure, and which talks of suffering as the result of our (or our mothers') inability to get things right. We do not need a fickle, obscure God who keeps us continually waiting to be punished for not having interpreted his wishes appropriately. Such a theology has a lot in common with the dynamics of domestic abuse!

A feminist theology, which takes seriously the uncalled-for suffering of women, needs to be able to respond to the suffering and dilemmas of choice with which genetic information (like other features of women's and men's lives) presents us, without imposing a burden of guilt. But it also needs to respond to the reality of a creation that is not always good.

God looked at what God had made, and it was good

It is possible to delight in the creation. Creation is indeed beautiful, a gift from God. But it is also wild, random, chaotic, powerful and destructive. How are we to understand a God whose world destroys as well as creates, causes grief and devastation as well as joy and delight? Creation may have looked good in God's eyes, but such an assessment is harder to make when one discovers that one and/or one's descendants must live with a life threatening and distressing genetic condition.

In reflecting upon how one understands choice, as a woman dealing with the dilemmas of genetic testing, I find myself drawn to Job. In the discussion that follows I draw heavily on the writing of Gutiérrez.[17] His work has always had a strong understanding of justice, and a strong critique of theology's ability to perpetuate

---

[17] Gustavo Gutiérrez, *The Power of the Poor in History* (London, SCM Press, 1983); Gustavo Gutiérrez, *We Drink from our own Wells* (Maryknoll, New York, Orbis Books, 1984); Gustavo Gutiérrez, *On Job: God-talk and the Suffering of the Innocent* (Maryknoll, New York, Orbis Books, 1987).

oppression and justify the position of the powerful. He takes seriously the reality of lived experience, and of uncalled-for suffering, which he calls the 'suffering of the innocent'. His community is that of the poor in South America, the non-person whose suffering seems endless. In his commentary on Job, Gutiérrez grapples with the problem of how to understand innocent suffering.

Job is the story of a successful, God-fearing person. Suddenly he is struck down by affliction, and cannot understand why this has happened to him. Yet, when invited to curse God, to speak ill of God, he does not do so. He rejects an understanding of his relationship with God that is based only on God's ability to give Job what he wants or deserves. Job does not accept a utilitarian religion, a relationship based on expectation of reward.

So too, as women confront their experience of patriarchal oppression, or the meaningless suffering of genetic illness, it is a temptation to speak ill of God. Like Job, we may be surrounded by people who despair of God, and who suggest that we blame God for the situation we are in, for the level of suffering, anguish, difficulty. But as Gutiérrez argues, what Job is called to is a disinterested religion, a relationship with God not based on God's ability to provide us with the goodness of life, or on our ability to manipulate God, but based instead on a disinterested self surrender to God.

This expectation of God as the rewarder of virtue and the punisher of disobedience, means that Job's family and friends cannot understand what is happening to Job, except in terms of sin. They sit with him in his suffering, and then try to convince Job that he must repent. Repent and all will be well, God will reward you. Job protests his innocence; he protests and resists their explanation. Job will not trade his innocence for a false guilt in order to make his experience fit the acceptable model of suffering. Job will not be seduced into that inadequate understanding of the basis of relationship with God. The equation of suffering with sin, the argument that suffering is a consequence of disobedience is not good enough. It does not fit Job's experience. He knows that he is innocent and will not accept a theology that does not make sense. 'Job's point of departure was both his own experience and his faith in the living God; it was on the basis of this that he challenged, and gradually dismantled, the doctrine of retribution that his three friends expounded...'.[18] As Job rejects the retributive God, and the theology offered by his friends, he finds common ground with the poor, and recognises his community of fellow-sufferers, those who are also innocent and cry out for justice. Job's protests move beyond protestations of his own innocence to recognition of the equality of all people. He continues to complain to God, to demand a response, and to call for justice. But his cry for justice is now not only for himself, but for all. Job recognises his common humanity, and asks God to respond to the needs of others as well.

It is notable that Job's conversation is not merely *about* God, but *to* God, and indeed that 'his full encounter with God comes by way of complaint, bewilderment and confrontation'.[19] So too, I argue, can women protest and resist the traditional analysis of the cause of their innocent suffering, and the inadequate understanding of God that is proclaimed in a theology limited to God as the all powerful (father) figure who must be obeyed... Such protestation and resistance can express itself in lament and protest, in argument with God, in questioning and debate. This is the tradition also found in the psalms. A theology that can permit such direct engagement with God assumes a different model of God – a resilient God who can cope with such conversation and not be threatened by it or feel the need to crush such direct confrontation. Such a God does not despise or belittle honesty and passion.

So there is room here for a resilient God, one with whom we are able to be honest, direct, confrontational. But this leaves the question unresolved; who is this God with whom we contest and argue? What sort of God creates a world where genetic disease happens, where oppression and injustice continues?

---

[18] Gutiérrez, *On Job*, p.47.
[19] Gutiérrez, *On Job*, p.55.

I'm not sure this can be resolved and kept tidy. Perhaps these questions, so similar to the ones with which Job struggled, are still a search for a God I can comprehend, control, predict. Perhaps I am still trying to reduce God to some sort of utilitarian relationship where I know how to maximise benefit for myself or for others.

And perhaps my struggles to cope with and understand a creation that does not always appear 'good' is a reflection of my own culture, which tends to see creation as something to meet our needs, malleable to our wishes and manipulations. So much of my western scientific culture is predicated on the understanding of the world as being for man's (and sometimes humanity's) benefit. My culture has largely reduced creation to a thing, an object or a machine. It has become something that we can pull apart to understand, use as we see fit, manipulate and control.[20] It is a challenge to let go all the assumptions written into that world view, and see creation as something of which humans are simply a part, and not the central figure, and to assess its goodness on the basis of something other than creation's utilitarian value to humans.

As Job struggles to understand his suffering, God points out that creation is not only for the benefit of humans. Creation is larger than Job can understand, and has purposes beyond humanity. Creation has value in and of itself, independent of the value that humans may place upon it.

The wonder of Job's engagement with God is that in the midst of God's speech to Job, in which all this is pointed out, God also invites humanity to collaborate in building a just world. But the justice spoken of is based on freedom, not coercion. God has demonstrated God's power, the majesty of creation which is more than Job can imagine. God has reminded Job that it is all beyond his understanding or comprehension. Yet, God does speak to Job, God does respond. Not on Job's terms or in line with his expectations, but nevertheless, God speaks. The God who has created the

---

[20] See Carolyn Merchant, *The Death of Nature* (San Francisco, Harper & Row, 1980).

entire world and set it on its foundations, speaks to Job, and offers him the possibility of participating in the continual creation of the world. It is the free gift of God, inviting and offering a relationship in freedom – rather than in coercion, or fear, or submission.

Job does not seem to understand God at the end. The relationship is not based on understanding, but more on awe, on the mystery of a God who offers relationship at all. It is a God we can never comprehend or understand or predict, but who invites us to freedom.

This is at heart a mystical understanding of God, in that it is given in terms that are untidy, unresolved. But it is an understanding that sees untidiness and incomprehensibility as a necessary part of a theology that refuses to reduce God to something that can be defined, predicted or understood. Rather we are left with a God with whom we can relate and lament and complain and celebrate.

For genetic testing, it seems to me, is both burden and blessing. Like so many medical and scientific advances it gives us the skills and ability to reduce human suffering, to bear healthy children. But it also gives us increased responsibility in an area where we are more accustomed to accept whatever life brings, however tragic, and to be resigned not to have control over this area of our lives. But now we have the possibility of control – and must express our choice in some way or another. Like the knowledge of nuclear power, it is not something that we can unlearn.

And choice can be frightening. How much easier, less complicated, to create a God who sets rules, rewards us when we get it right, punishes us when we get it wrong. Such a God can be attractive – it offers (we may think) security and hope, peace and healthy children, avoidance of pain and dilemma. It is just unfortunate that it is an understanding of God that is so unhelpful in responding to our experiences of un-called for suffering, and unavoidable and difficult choice.

Practical implications

As genetic testing becomes more frequent, and even routine, it will increasingly become one of the rituals of motherhood, part of the process of giving (or not giving) birth. At times the results will be a source of relief, or may be so routine and reassuring that tests during subsequent pregnancies can be taken for granted, no more important than a blood test to confirm one has immunity to rubella. But on other occasions genetic test results will be earth shattering, calling for an expression of one's human freedom and responsibility in a dramatic way, presenting women with dilemmas for which there are no unambiguous resolutions. In such a situation, women will be looking for ways of making meaning of their experience and choice; of understanding how life can be like this, and why they choose whatever choice they make; they must find a way to live with their decision, whatever it is, and whatever grief or burden or relief they may feel.

Yet currently the experience is hidden, private, and frequently unsupported. Women speak of not telling anyone they are pregnant until the test results are back and the decisions are made, and of not even acknowledging the movement of the baby until they can be confident that they will be continuing with the pregnancy.[21]

The public discourse about God is important here, in helping women make sense of the choices they face, and the unfriendly and tragic forces of nature. The uncritical re-production of dominant theological discourses about women (the submission of Mary and the disobedience of Eve) reproduces a burden of guilt or inadequacy that is neither appropriate nor helpful. Women who are faced with these choices cannot be blamed for the genetic conditions they carry. But they do need some way to understand the nature of the choice that is before them.

Deconstructing traditional patriarchal theology is not the same as constructing an alternative. Uncovering the bias and burden of dominant theology is only a beginning. But it is an important step on the way to finding a theology that heals and liberates. Being liberated from a burden of guilt for innocent suffering is an important step. Articulating an understanding of a God who does not seek to control us through reward and punishment but invites us to

---

[21] See Rothman, *The Tentative Pregnancy*.

an encounter in complaint, bewilderment and confrontation – well, even Job found that a challenge!

The challenge that genetic testing presents to me is how to talk of God in the face of a creation that does not appear good, and how to understand and talk of God in the face of the choices with which women are now being presented. We cannot 'unlearn' knowledge. We may, over the next few decades, develop some consensus about some aspects of genetic information, but it is more likely that responses will continue to vary between individuals, families and communities. But we will need to find ways to learn to live with this knowledge. Women will need to, are needing to, find ways to make sense of the new choices that they now face. Understandings of reproduction, genetics and science are as riddled with patriarchal assumptions as is theology. Practical feminist theology has some interesting conversations ahead as it explores the implications of technical advances for women and for our communities.

IX

The subject and practice of pastoral theology as a practical theological discipline: pushing past the nagging identity crisis to the poetics of resistance

Bonnie J. MILLER-MCLEMORE

To identify the existential subject of pastoral theology, many scholars in the United States hearken back to Anton Boisen's foundational metaphor. Distinct from other areas of religious study, the object is *'the study of living human documents rather than books'*.[1] Elsewhere I have critiqued the individualistic leanings of this metaphor and its focus on the 'separative' self as a singular document rather than the 'connective' self as participatory and the weave of the wider context.[2] And I suggest an alternative, related image: to study religion in pastoral theology is to study the living web. I do not think it too exaggerated to say that further reflection on the subject and practice of pastoral theology as a practical theological discipline is needed now more than ever before.

---

[1] Anton Boisen, (1950), cited by Charles Gerkin, *The Living Human Document: Revisioning Pastoral Counseling in a Hermeneutical Mode* (Nashville, Abingdon, 1973, 1984), p. 37.

[2] Bonnie J. Miller-McLemore, 'The Human Web and the State of Pastoral Theology', *Christian Century* (April 7, 1993), pp. 366-69 and 'The Living Human Web: Pastoral Theology at the Turn of the Century' in Jeanne Stevenson Moessner (ed.), *Through the Eyes of Women: Insights for Pastoral Care* (Philadelphia, Westminster/John Knox, 1996), pp. 9-26. See also Catherine Keller, *From a Broken Web. Separation, Sexism, and Self* (Boston, Beacon, 1986).

The persistent identity crisis

Compared to many areas in the study of religion, religion and personality – a name used by some academic programs in the United States to encompass the many facets of the field that includes pastoral theology – is strikingly young. So, for example, Vanderbilt University Divinity School added its first full-time faculty member in the area of pastoral counseling in 1959. The position was defined in relation to psychology and the medical school around counseling as a special ministerial skill alongside administration, preaching, and communications. Whereas biblical studies in the United States formed its earliest academic society in the late 1800s, pastoral theology did not begin to gather its members into a distinct organization until after the middle of this century. In 1984 The Association of Practical Theology (APT) was formed, partially under the influence of Don Browning. And in 1985 the Society for Pastoral Theology (SPT) was initially convened by Liston Mills and James Lapsley. Both organizations attempted to address concerns not adequately met through a slightly older organization, The Association of Seminary Professors in the Practical Fields (ASPPF). The ASPPF had been established by Ross Snyder and Seward Hiltner in the 1950s and became the Association of Professional Education for Ministry in the 1970s in an attempt to widen its membership beyond seminary education and the 'practical' fields before disbanding in 1982.[3]

To push these examples a bit further, initially the American Association of Pastoral Counselors, an organization for the certification of therapists and an important part of the pastoral theology movement in the 1960s and 1970s, felt threatened by the revival of the SPT because it would inevitably draw academics away. And in the last few years the APT has had a revival of its own which will in turn, I believe, challenge the numbers and strength of the SPT. Certainly the creation of the International Academy of Practical

---

[3] Some of this history of the organizations has been recounted to me by colleagues Herbert Anderson and Liston Mills.

Theology in 1992 promises both to increase the visibility of certain facets of the discipline *and* to siphon off energies formerly devoted more narrowly to pastoral theology.

Meanwhile, many United States scholars in the general area of religion and personality, particularly those in universities and colleges, do not see either of these organizations as primary. They work more explicitly in the area of religious studies and are likely to attend the American Academy of Religion or the Social Scientific Study of Religion. Some pastoral theologians attempt to maintain an allegiance to these organizations as well.

During the past century, professional guilds have come to wield a power over religion – how it is studied and taught in the United States – that is seldom recognized, studied, or understood. However, the point of these extended examples at the moment is rather simple: although in one sense predecessors in the field date back to Kierkegaard, Luther, Catholic moral theology, Augustine, even Jewish rabbinical counsel and early house-church movements, in another sense the current area of religion and personality does not know any pre-scientific, pre-Enlightenment, pre-modern period, before which its study of religion was not influenced by rational, scientific methods. In a sense, pastoral theology is a modern study of religion *par excellence*, coming to fruition precisely as a result of new so-called objective, measurable, empirical means of knowing the 'truths' of human experience. In other words, the field did not consolidate its academic position until after the social sciences, psychology in particular, had given new life to the study of the person, religious experience, pastoral care and ministry. In some settings the field was organized around a narrow model of professional training. Moreover, just as the field might have begun to consolidate its parameters and assumptions about the study of religion, modern models of knowing and truth began to fall apart. Hence, unity, values and facts in the study of religion are challenged anew by post-modern understandings of truth as contextual, culture-bound, value-loaded, subjective, allusive, and so on. How could a movement become established in a context where established disciplines of religious and theological studies themselves were under fire?

So, on the one hand, the modern psychologies of Freud, James, Jung and others, gave lifeblood to the study of religion in theological schools and clinical settings and led to a powerful new movement of religion and personality and the renewal of pastoral theology, care, counseling, psychotherapy and, most recently, spiritual direction. On the other, the movement was split right from the beginning.

This split is perhaps best exemplified in the diverse names by which those who work in the general area of religion and personality identify what they do: those in the area may teach psychology of religion, sociology of religion, religion and personality, religion and culture, pastoral care, pastoral counseling, pastoral psychology, pastoral theology, practical theology, religion and psychology, and most recently, ethics or moral theology. As these titles reflect, the practice of the discipline in the United States can be roughly divided into three groups: those involved in the empirical or hermeneutical social scientific study of religious experience, those interested in practical and pastoral theology, care, and counseling, and those engaged in the critical personal and cultural correlation of theology and the social sciences.

Where one stands within this three-fold classification partially corresponds to the location of one's primary work in seminary or university-related divinity school or college and university. It also partially corresponds to the location of one's work in relation to the recent and complex distinction between and debate about theological studies and religious studies. On this score it is interesting to note that teaching in the field within a university-situated divinity school, as distinct from a free-standing seminary or a department of religion in a university or college, presents unique challenges by forcing careful attention to the dual commitments of the academic study of religion *and* the professional training of ministers who profess faith. It is in such a context that I seek further insight into the nature of the discipline of pastoral theology.

My own research on the subjects of families, mothers, work, love, and death and dying has tended to fall into the two categories of practical, pastoral theology and critical correlation of religion and culture, reflecting both where I have come to teach and my own scholarly interests.[4] However, as a feminist pastoral theologian I identify the critical correlation of religion and culture as an essential component of an adequate practical, pastoral theology. The important point for the moment, however, is less my own particular approach. Rather the point is: anyone who wants to write a comprehensive text in the general area of religion and personality must first address and in some fashion dispel the persistent identity crisis of the field or at least situate one's work in relation to this crisis. This also means addressing the conflicts in the study of religion more broadly speaking. And given the nature of the academic debate over matters of religious beliefs and the pursuit of knowledge, neither of these tasks promises an easy entrance into the discussion.

Bellowing through the darkness: rudimentary definitions

My beginning proposition about how one studies religion in the general area of religion and personality studies, and pastoral theology within that area, is simple, even if its practice issues in terribly complex questions, forms, and problems: one studies religion at the point where human suffering evokes or calls for a religious response and sometimes at the point where a religious response is given and/or experienced. As black feminist bell hooks puts it, one dares 'to create theory from the location of pain and struggle'. Indeed, she expresses her gratitude to those who so risk, for 'it is not easy to name our pain, to theorize from that location'; it takes courage to 'expose wounds' and to lend one's experience as a 'means to chart new theoretical journeys'.[5] In a poem that picks up the metaphor of weave and web, 'Needle/Plow,' Barbara Seaman captures some of what happens among scholars in religion and

---

[4] Bonnie J. Miller-McLemore, *Death, Sin and the Moral Life: Contemporary Cultural Interpretations of Death and Dying* (Atlanta, Scholars, 1988); *Also A Mother: Work and Family as Theological Dilemma* (Nashville, Abingdon, 1994).

[5] bell hooks [Gloria Watkins], *Teaching to Transgress: Education as the Practice of Freedom* (New York, Routledge & Kegan Paul, 1994), p. 74.

personality and pastoral theology.[6] 'Knowing how to pull a straight line will help, but it's depth,' she says, 'that matters – being willing to push through the obvious weave of the world to the underview ... that and not being afraid to belly through darkness ...'

Measured against this definition, sometimes the best pastoral theology does not evolve from those who call themselves pastoral theologians. Church historian Roberta Bondi's work is a wonderful case in point. Protesting against the ways both the repressive images of an authoritarian God in her confessional Baptist background and the objective abstractions of her higher academic education distort the Christian theological enterprise, she redefines 'the primary stuff of theology'. Theology is about the 'messy particularity of everyday lives examined with excruciating care and brought into conversation with the great doctrines of the Christian tradition'.[7] And while bell hooks would not identify herself as a pastoral theologian, when her efforts to address the sufferings and healing of African-American women lead her to emphasize the wisdom of the elders, the movement of the spirit and the resources of religious traditions and communities despite their occasional hypocrisy, then she qualifies as such.[8]

If a comprehensive orientation distinguishes the area of religion and personality and pastoral theology within it, it is the focus on living, rather than dead persons and cultures, the focus on the psyche, whether understood as ego, soul, or self, and the focus on the clinical or therapeutic or healing dimension of psyche and living persons.[9]

In the last decade or so, under the influence of many kinds of liberation theology, especially feminist theologies, these three foci

---

[6] Barbara Seaman, *The Christian Century*, (November 6, 1996), p. 1062.

[7] Paul Slentz, student book report on *Memories of God: Theological Reflections on a Life* by Roberta C. Bondi, (Nashville, Abingdon, 1995)

[8] See bell hooks, *Sisters of the Yam: Black Women and Self-Recovery* (Boston, South End, 1993).

[9] I acknowledge my colleague in Hebrew Bible, Douglas Knight, for this characterization during a colloquium in which I presented parts of this chapter.

have engendered a fourth related interest in the political dimension of healing that sees a prophetic, social, proactive stance as imperative for pastoral theology. Beyond the conventional modes of healing, sustaining, guiding, and reconciling of William Clebsch and Charles Jaekle with which pastoral care has been routinely equated, the intent becomes resisting, empowering, nurturing, and liberating.[10]

Although significantly influenced by other contemporary theological movements, this political imperative in pastoral theology is not simply a borrowing from other areas of study in religion, but is foreshadowed within the field itself. An emphasis on political and social freedom has roots among the early founders of the movement such as Boisen and Hiltner who were themselves influenced by Erich Fromm and the Frankfurt School of social theory.[11] One could feasibly argue that even the common title of religion and personality signals broader interests than a focus on the individual psyche since it borrows from anthropology the term of 'personality' as always culturally reflexive and constructed. Furthermore, this suggests that a better comprehensive title for the area might be religion, personality *and culture*.

Notably, this fourth focus signals a rapprochement between the work in pastoral theology and the work in other fields besides Bondi in church history, such as the work in systematic theology by Catherine Keller, Rita Nakashima Brock, Marjorie Suchocki, and others. As postmodernism and liberation movements challenge basic definitions of truth and reality, others in the field of religion have themselves become more interdisciplinary and anthropological in their approaches. Understanding lived subjective experience becomes an important means of mapping the mak-

---

[10] Partially based on Carroll Weaver's informal remarks during a panel at the American Academy of Religion, November 1996, drawing on her dissertation work on womanist pastoral theology. See William Clebsch and Charles Jaekle, *Pastoral Care in Historical Perspective*, 2d. ed. (New York: Aronson, 1983).

[11] Rodney J. Hunter, 'The Therapeutic Tradition of Pastoral Care and Counseling,' in Pamela D. Couture and Rodney J. Hunter, (eds.), *Pastoral Care and Social Conflict* (Nashville, Abingdon, 1995), p. 20.

ing and unmaking of culture in a variety of religious disciplines.[12] If God is seen as located within the other and within the outcast and dispossessed, than students in a variety of previously distinct disciplines of religious studies must develop fresh ways to relate and focus on the other. If 'postmodernism signals not an absolute breaking-up of the hegemony of modern Western culture'[13] but a receptivity to other perspectives and values as part of the complex constellation that comprises human life, then scholars in pastoral theology join others in adopting a notably postmodern, deconstructivist tone and method while harboring residual modern faiths and hopes.

It is also important to note briefly the convergence and divergence of pastoral and practical theology which the three-fold classification above lumps perhaps too carelessly into one group. Recognition of the importance of pastoral theology as distinctly focused on particular human anguish and responses makes me wary of too quick a move from pastoral theology into the broader or more comprehensive realm of practical theology as one means to retain a foothold in the academy. And in some cases, academic survival is precisely what deliberations about practical theology seem to have as their agenda. Practical theology, perhaps because it sometimes can operate at a greater level of abstraction and theoretical generalization than pastoral theology, seems to obtain thereby some kind of scholarly validity. But this validity, just as the organizations in the example above, remains precarious due to practical theology's unavoidable interests and even confessional commitments to the church and faith itself. In addition, abstraction and objectivity have been used to obscure and silence other perceptions and truths. In a postmodern context, one must wonder about the adequacy of a discipline predicated on modernist scientific values.

Nonetheless, a practical theological methodology remains critical and useful, less in and of itself, and more in approaching and

---

[12] Remarks by Paula Cooey, 'Theological Anthropology After Modernism', The American Academy of Religion, New Orleans, November 1996.

[13] Maureen Dallison Kemeza, 'Dante as Guide and Provocation,' *Christian Century* 113, no. 34 (November 20-27, 1996), p. 1148.

constructing particular submovements, including those of pastoral care, religious education, liturgical studies, and so forth. So, to attend and respond to human distress in pastoral theology, I use practical theological steps – commonly identified by scholars such as Don Browning, Thomas Groome, James and Evelyn Whitehead and others – of descriptive understanding, comparative analysis in dialogical conversation with religious and secular resources, evaluation, and decision.

Illustrative readings in the weave of the world

To develop the idea that one studies religion in pastoral theology at the point where human suffering evokes or calls for a religious response and sometimes at the point where a religious response is given and/or experienced, I turn to three selected readings from Augustine, Boisen, and my own book, *Also A Mother*. I offer these readings as purely illustrative and without explicit analysis, prior to making some suggestive generalizations. I want to move readers into direct engagement with the difficult and complex task at hand when studying religion in pastoral theology, by locating concretely the study of religion in diverse moments of suffering from which religious reflection, and perhaps theology, emerges or has emerged. Having done that, rather than analyze any one of these readings, I will make three general observations about the study of religion in pastoral theology and conclude with a brief identification of some of the problems and possibilities. The illustrative selections from texts are mostly random; any number of readings – C. S. Lewis' *A Grief Observed*; womanist essays on suffering and evil in *A Troubling in My Soul*; recent stories of the struggles of gay men and lesbians in *Wrestling with Angels* – could serve this purpose.[14] However, the readings from Augustine

---

[14] C. S. Lewis, *A Grief Observed* (New York, Bantam, 1961); Emilie Townes, (ed.), *A Troubling in My Soul: Womanist Perspectives on Evil and Suffering* (Maryknoll, NY, Orbis, 1993); and Brian Bouldrey, *Wrestling with the Angel: Faith and Religion in the Lives of Gay Men* (New York, Riverhead Book, 1995).

and Boisen represent pivotal voices that have shaped the field. I include *Also A Mother* to demonstrate some of the changing parameters of the field and my work within it. Any number of selections from the texts could be used; I merely chose one reading from many that embody acute moments of struggle.

A corollary intent behind inserting these voices, unanalyzed, into this chapter, is to evoke through them echoes of each person's own moments of encounter with what David Tracy calls 'limit situations', from which almost all interest in the study of religion flows regardless of the eventual form that religious study takes.[15] To a greater extent than other areas of religious studies, religion and personality studies in general, and pastoral theology more specifically, make limit situations a central focus. My hope in this chapter is not just to come to an understanding of how scholars, myself included, work in the sometimes boundary-less field of religion and personality studies, but to spark each reader's own reflection of her own work within the study of religion. Rather than analyze each reading as a limit situation from which further religious and theological reflection emerges, several observations about the nature of religious study in pastoral theology will be made with these illustrative moments in the background.

Reading 1:

> And I, as I looked back over my life, was quite amazed to think of how long a time had passed since my nineteenth year, when I had first become inflamed with a passion for wisdom ... now I was in my thirtieth year, still sticking in the same mud, still greedy for the enjoyment of things present, which fled from me and wasted me away, and all the time saying: I shall find it tomorrow. See, it will become quite clear and I shall grasp it ... But where shall I look for it? And when shall I look for it? ... And where can I find the books? From where can I get them and when can I get them? Can I borrow them from anybody? ...

[15] David Tracy, *Blessed Rage for Order: The New Pluralism in Theology* (New York, Seabury, 1975), pp. 93, 104-08.

But these are not the thoughts I should have ... Life is a misery, death an uncertainty. Suppose it steals suddenly upon me, in what state shall I leave this world? ... Shall I be punished for my negligence? Or is it true that death will cut off and put an end to all care and all feeling? ... So I used to speak and so the winds blew and shifted and drove my heart this way and that, and time went by and I was slow in turning ... (Augustine, *The Confessions*)[16]

Reading 2:

While working one day on the Statement of Belief – I think it was Wednesday, October 6 – some strange ideas came surging into my mind, ideas of doom, ideas of my own unsuspected importance. With them began the frank psychosis ... It began without evidence of undue exaltation ...[but then] Everything began to whirl. It seemed that the world was coming to an end ...
... As I look back upon the strange ideas which came flooding into my mind during the disturbed periods ... [I see that] the sufferer is striving desperately to face what for him is ultimate Reality. Thus interpreted, an acute schizophrenic episode assumes the character of religious experience. It becomes an attempt at thoroughgoing reorganization, beginning at the very center of one's being, an attempt which tends either to make or break the personality. (Anton T. Boisen, *Out of the Depths*)[17]

Reading 3:

Resolution of the daily conflicts [of family and paid work] leads inevitably to contradictions, frustrations, ambiguous solutions, and hard choices. One day while trying to revise a manuscript during the naptime of one of my sons, I recall feeling torn between my desire for total uninterrupted silence and horror at my fantasy that a capricious god might grant me my impulsive wish and I would lose my children forever ... A hundred times – and not for the last time by any means – I have wondered, am I attempting a self-defeating feat, trying to 'conceive' in professional and familial ways at the same time? ...

---

[16] *The Confessions of St. Augustine*, translated by Rex Warner (New York, Mentor, 1963), pp. 127-29.
[17] *Out of the Depths: An Autobiographical Study of Mental Disorder and Religious Experience* (New York, Harper & Brothers, 1960), pp. 79-83, 205.

... Having children forever changed my way of knowing and thinking about generativity. Parting the passions to articulate in what ways comes less easily ... How might we systematically conceptualize this maternal knowing that in [Mary] Gordon's words is more physical and certainly more erotic 'than anybody admits'? ... As point of proof, what does it mean to lactate, to have a body that, sensing another's thirst, 'lets-down', drenching me with sweet-smelling milk? Does it alter knowing?

... In the movement between the knowing and acting of nursing and tending an infant, I use a mode of circular bodily reasoning, interweaving physical sensation, momentary cognition, behavioral reaction, and a physical sensing and intellectual reading of the results – a trial and error, hit-and-miss strategy, which in its bodily ethos, surpasses that described under the rubric of Catholic moral casuistry ... In contrast to the hierarchy of knowledge that ranks rational above other forms, we know much in and through our bodies that is intrinsically valuable and precious ...

... Maternal generativity begins to suggest a way to understand the problem of integrating praxis and theory better than almost anything I have seen in the current literature of practical theology. It challenges false dichotomies: Theory does not involve simply verbalizable knowledge and insight, as much as many have wished. Practice does not mean unmediated action. Both involve qualities more nebulous, fleeting, relative, and momentary. Theory involves the passing recognition of empathic attunement; practice, movement within the realm of attuned theory. (Miller-McLemore, *Also A Mother*, pp. 31, 146-49)[18]

Refusing the pretense of objectivity

The following observations are not meant to be comprehensive. They are, in fact, hard to organize. As one way to do so, I rely on a quote from Mary K. DeShazer's book, *A Poetics of Resistance: Women Writing in El Salvador, South Africa, and the United States*, cited by Christine Smith in an essay on preaching. According to DeShazer, poetry participates in resistance in at least three ways: 1) poems 'refuse the pretense of objectivity'; 2) they 'vio-

---

[18] *Also A Mother*, pp. 30-32, 146-49.

late poetic decorum in order to invite conflict and confrontation';
and finally, 3) they 'call forth from their audience an alternative
complicity, a willingness to participate in a re-visionary project –
ethical, political, literary – that could actually make a difference in
the lives of the marginalized'.[19] The study of religion in pastoral
theology has many qualities, but these three capture assumptions
in its modern history that have become more pronounced in our
time of post-modernity.

De Shazer argues that poems of resistance 'refuse the pretense
of objectivity, instead asserting polemically the terms of their
engagement with the topic at hand. In so doing, they claim as their
own the task of historiographic reconstruction.'[20] Recognizing the
pretense of objectivity and identifying one's particular context and
perspective characterizes the work of many current scholars in
pastoral theology more than those in religion and personality
engaged in the social scientific study of religious experience. But
it presents challenges to both parties. With the hermeneutic of suspicion as defined by Elisabeth Schüssler Fiorenza, conscious partiality is sought rather than objectivity, participation replaces spec-
tator knowledge, the starting point is to change the status quo, and
research is a process of consciousness-raising that assists
women.[21]

To study religion from this vantage point then means to engage
in a power analysis of the biases behind the construction of theories about human nature, not unlike that now engaged in by some
biblical scholars studying scriptural texts. Power analysis entails
an investigation into and deconstruction of the framework that
defines the context and nature of suffering and a reconstruction of

---

[19] Mary K. DeShazer, *A Poetics of Resistance: Women Writing in El Salvador,
South Africa, and the United States* (Ann Arbor: University of Michigan Press,
1994), p. 271, cited by Christine M. Smith, 'Preaching as an Art of Resistance,' in
Christie Cozad Neuger (ed.), *The Arts of Ministry: Feminist-Womanist Approaches*
(Louisville, Westminster/John Knox, 1996), p. 47.

[20] De Shazer, *A Poetics of Resistance*, p. 47.

[21] Cited by Judith Orr, 'Administration as an Art of Shared Vision,' in
Christie Cozad Neuger (ed.), *The Arts of Ministry: Feminist-Womanist Approaches*
(Louisville, Westminster/John Knox, 1996), p. 138.

the nature of suffering from alternative standpoints. Human suffering then is not defined simply along individual psychological lines. It calls for new psychological and religious understandings that take into account the social, political, and religious contexts of suffering. Echoing an early women's movement slogan that the personal is political, personal *suffering* is political.

When 'truths' about religious ideas such as sin or servanthood or love are relocated within alternative subjectivities, suddenly other understandings become apparent. For example, as many feminist theologians have elaborated since Valerie Saiving's classic 1960s essay, 'sin' is not always or necessarily pridefulness or will to power or assertion or misuse of one's freedom. When the temptation to sin is experienced in other contexts, certainly that of some women and those with fewer choices and less freedom, the temptation comes as the lure of self-dispersion, relentless self-castigation, fragmentation, loss of voice, and loss of self in life's endless details. Or, as another example, the idea of 'servanthood' as Christian ideal takes on new meanings when womanist Jacqueline Grant claims a particular subjectivity and context. It matters historically, in the United States context of slavery and its aftermath, she asserts, that some folk have been 'more servant than others.' The theme of servanthood can be retained *only* if it means to join 'in the struggle of the redeemer against oppression, wherever it is found' as servants of the liberator Jesus.[22] Or, to take one last instance, Protestant definitions of the ideal of human love as self-sacrificial *agape* tend to distort and abort the struggles among those previously silenced and marginalized. Sociologist of religion Cheryl Townsend Gilkes concludes an essay about the ways in which dominant cultural norms of beauty undercut the self-esteem of African-American women with a dialectical understanding of self-love and love of others. At this moment in history, 'Self-love then is probably the most critical task we complete in establishing

---

[22] Jacquelyn Grant, 'The Sin of Servanthood,' in Emilie Townes (ed.), *A Troubling in My Soul: Womanist Perspectives on Evil and Suffering* (Maryknoll, NY, Orbis, 1993), pp. 204, 213.

our commitment "to survival and wholeness of entire people, male and female"'.[23] New candidly subjective contexts mean new definitions in religion and personality. These are voices to be taken seriously precisely in their concrete particularities and contextual subjectivity.

This creates a bit of turmoil around a key thematic term in the field: empathy. Sparked by Carl Rogers' idea of unconditional positive regard, further refined within object-relations theory and Kohutian self-psychology, and used within a variety of venues in religion and personality, empathy has operated as both a prominent method of knowing and a critical aspect of human responsiveness. Yet the extent and capacity of empathy is now under some question. Scholars and practitioners can no longer assume that with proper psychological technique – analysis, mirroring, interpretation – or with proper religious studies technique – cultural anthropology, interdisciplinary investigation, phenomenology, hermeneutics – one can finally know the 'other' in the study of religion. As I argue in 'The Living Human Web', empathy is confounded by its limitations. 'Sometimes a person must admit an inability to fully understand the lived reality of the oppressions suffered by another. There may be boundaries beyond which empathy itself cannot go'.[24]

The goal shifts then from understanding *qua* understanding to connectivity in difference. Relationality as simply connectedness no longer suffices; relationality now means particularity and differentness as well as connectedness.[25] David Tracy lends theoretical support for this shift in his work on religion in a postmodern age of plurality and ambiguity: 'Empathy is much too romantic a category to comprehend this necessary movement in interpretation

---

[23] Cheryl Townsend Gilkes, 'The 'Loves' and 'Troubles' of African-American Women's Bodies,' in Emilie Townes (ed.), *A Troubling in My Soul: Womanist Perspectives on Evil and Suffering* (Maryknoll, NY, Orbis, 1993), p. 247.

[24] Bonnie J. Miller-McLemore, 'The Living Human Web,' p. 21.

[25] Carol Hess, 'Education as an Art of Getting Dirty with Dignity,' in Christie Cozad Neuger (ed.), *The Arts of Ministry: Feminist-Womanist Approaches* (Louisville, Westminster/John Knox, 1996), p. 65.

from otherness, to possibility, to similarity-in-difference'.[26] The intent in practical theology in listening to voices distinctly different from our own, according to Smith, is 'to move more fully and faithfully into what those difference can mean for all of us'. These 'holy places of difference ... challenge and terrify' rather than enlighten the listener.[27] To discern the true and the good in religion requires not just dialogue, but something a bit more elusive, that practical theologian Carol Hess calls 'hard dialogue' – difficult, painful questions, awareness of one's personal and cultural biases, and interaction with difference.

Violating religious and theological decorum

DeShazer asserts that poems of resistance 'violate poetic decorum in order to invite conflict and confrontation. They express anger ... they hammer readers with ... fierce rhetoric questions designed to evoke discomfort'. Contrary to the supposition that religion can be defined, systematized, or made coherent, to study religion in pastoral theology is to confront the limitations of imposed frameworks. The intent of the study is to get at the inexpressible without losing a genuine sense of it – much like prayer or poetry. Pastoral theology violates religious and theological decorum by claiming theology as messy and by assuming a face-to-face starting point.

The attempt to give order and coherence is not wrong in and of itself, but only as it stifles questions, hides human fallibility, or limits the range of questions and answers to its own order. In the art of education, Hess argues,

> There is nothing wrong with the systematic presentation of tradition and belief, especially in a time when there is so little knowledge of the tradition. There is something drastically wrong, how-

[26] David, Tracy, *Pluralism and Ambiguity: Hermeneutics, Religion and Hope* (San Francisco, Harper & Row, 1987), pp. 20-21.

[27] Christine M. Smith, 'Preaching as an Art of Resistance,' in Christie Cozad Neuger (ed.), *The Arts of Ministry: Feminist-Womanist Approaches* (Louisville, Westminster/John Knox, 1996), pp. 52, 56.

ever, with approaches to teaching that do not foster the type of question and depth conversation that is necessary for growth in theological maturity.[28]

Adequate theological method in practical theology must attend to the 'messy, dirty, earthy side of life': 'life lived in engagement with this world, is messy, conflicted, rough, dynamic, and weather-beaten'.[29] Presentational teaching or lectures then have a place only if they invite 'backtalk'. This metaphor from hooks in *Talking Back: Thinking Feminist, Thinking Black*, calls to mind a style of preaching and teaching that depends on participatory response, encouragement, engagement, and correction.[30] Academic scholarship in pastoral theology is clearly less interactive and more static than this, but nonetheless works better with an evocative, open-ended, less than conclusive, back-talk style that invites the listener into conversation. In this vein, writings that employ taped conversations, such as the final chapter on communion in *Setting the Table* or *God's Fierce Whimsey*, can have a more powerful or more memorable impact on the reader than a systematic presentation of the same ideas.

In *Lift Every Voice*, an edited collection of liberation 'theologies from the underside', Susan Thistlethwaite has a taped and transcribed dialogue with Mary Pellauer about grace and healing in the midst of violence against women – a topic about which Pellauer cannot bring herself to sit down and write. Pellauer observes,

> We're giving people messages about the meaning of theology –for instance, that is primarily written and not oral. But our experience over the last twenty years has been that it has been in face-to-face conversations that we have learned to do theology in a new way ... theology is not nearly so static as we may have thought when we read the final products in books or essays.

---

[28] Carol Hess, 'Education as an Art of Getting Dirty,' in Christie Cozad Neuger (ed.), *The Arts of Ministry: Feminist-Womanist Approaches* (Louisville, Westminster/ John Knox, 1996), pp. 75-76.

[29] Hess, 'Education as an Art of Getting Dirty', pp. 75-76.

[30] bell hooks, *Talking Back: Thinking Black, Thinking Black* (Boston: South End Press, 1989).

Later in the conversation, she notes, 'theology is not like mathematics, it's not a discipline for young persons at the end of adolescence. It's a discipline in which you need *time* to experience and to live with some insights, so you know what they mean over the long run'.[31]

Current work in pastoral theology draws on liberation theology partly because there are distinct affinities in particular methods that violate academic decorum. Liberation theologian Otto Maduro identifies three premises in liberation studies: 1) ordinary human life has precedence over 'doing theology'; 2) all theology is theology of specific life experience and attempts to respond to particular, not universal experience; and 3) theology is a result of 'life in community, shared faith, multiple efforts'.[32] The hoped-for intent, I would add, is to find 'classic' expressions, as Tracy describes them, of the particular that point beyond themselves to hints of more broadly shared experiences.

Practical theologian Don S. Browning makes a related argument for a new starting point for theological studies. The starting point is not biblical studies, historical studies, theological studies and then practical studies as in the nineteenth-century ordering of theological study that characterizes the discipline. Our contemporary turmoil within these categories seems to reflect a paradigm-shift waiting to happen. The starting point is what Browning calls 'fundamental practical theology' with historical theology, systematic theology, and ''strategic' practical theology' as moments within this more inclusive framework.

This framework stresses the priority of practical interests in the formation of our cognitive and moral world. Hans-Georg Gadamer and others argue that practical application shapes from the beginning theoretical questions. Rather than concern with practice as an act

---

[31] Mary D. Pellauer with Susan Brooks Thistlethwaite, 'Conversation on Grace and Healing: Perspectives from the Movement to End Violence Against Women,' in Susan Brooks Thistlethwaite and Mary Potter Engel (eds.), *Lift Every Voice: Constructing Theologies from the Underside*, (New York, Harper & Row, 1990), pp. 170, 175.

[32] Otto Maduro (1992), cited by Lallene Rector, unpublished manuscript.

that follows understanding or the application of theory to the specifics of praxis, 'concern with practice, in subtle ways we often overlook' guides the hermeneutic process from the beginning.[33] In a sense, one moves from theory-laden practice to practice-laden theory back to theory-laden practice.

The problem of the 'clerical paradigm' – that is, the focus on techniques of professional ministry as the main subject of modern practical theology – is partially due to the limited horizons of the practical theological fields and the obsession with technical training in counseling skills. But the problem is not only a problem *within* the field; it is also a larger systemic issue. The problem of the 'clerical paradigm' is also a result of the movement of systematic and construction theology away from the messiness of human suffering, the complications of religious and ministerial practices, and the ambiguities of faith claims and spiritual experiences. Schleiermacher's efforts succeeded in securing a place for theology in the university, but they came at a cost. Not only did he tend to see theology as reflection on ministerial expertise. The establishment of theology as a university discipline also subjected theology to singular external scientific, rationalistic standards of knowledge that ignore other '"habits of attention," "provinces of meaning," and "modes of experience"' and sometimes remove it from vital sources in religious faith and practice.[34]

Browning's approach, as the method in liberation theology, has other historical precedents in Roman Catholic theology, in pragmatic philosophy, in empirical theology. In her book on *Body, Sex, and Pleasure*, Catholic ethicist Christine Gudorf, for example, asserts that the first step in reconstructing Christian sexual ethics is not to begin with particular traditions, scriptures, or doctrinal faith statements, but 'to understand as best we can human sexuality itself, and in this day and age this means consulting both biological science as well as the experience of human individuals and

---

[33] Don S. Browning, *A Fundamental Practical Theology: Descriptive and Strategic Proposals* (Minneapolis, Fortress, 1991), pp. 7-8.

[34] See Martin E. Marty, 'The Modes of Being, Doing, and Teaching, and Discovering,' *Criterion* 35, no. 2 (Spring/Summer 1996), pp. 25-36.

communities'. We need to 'begin doing ethics with a description of the reality of our situation'. Once done, then we can turn to reflections on the religious dimensions or theological reflection on the meaning and significance of what has been described.[35]

In an emphasis on the messiness of face-to-face encounter, poetry, prayer, psychoanalytic understanding of religion, and pastoral theology are at least united in this one premise about expressing the inexpressible: 'under each speech is an underlying text written on the threshold of the unconscious'.[36] Each practitioner – poet, mystic, analyst, pastor/scholar – is willing, in the words of my introductory poem, 'to push through the obvious weave of the world to the underview, always turning the surface over like looking at both sides of an argument'.

Calling forth participation

Finally, DeShazer contends that poems of resistance 'call forth from their audience an alternative complicity, a willingness to participate in a re-visionary project – ethical, political, literary – that could actually make a difference in the lives of the marginalized'.[37] One studies religion by standing at the point where human suffering evokes or calls for a religious response and sometimes at the point where religious response is given or experienced. For many scholars in religion and personality, working from the vantage point of suffering necessarily entails a proactive starting point. The intent is to break silences, to challenge the status quo, to participate in what womanist theologian Emilie Towns calls, the 'radical truth telling' required by an ethic of justice and love.

---

[35] Christine E. Gudorf, *Body, Sex, and Pleasure: Reconstructing Christian Sexual Ethics* (Cleveland, Pilgrim, 1994), pp. 3-5.

[36] Ralph L. Underwood, *Pastoral Care and the Means of Grace* (Minneapolis, Fortress Press, 1993), p. 30.

[37] Mary K. DeShazer, *A Poetics of Resistance: Women writing in El Salvador, South Africa, and the United States* (Ann Arbor, University of Michigan Press, 1994), p. 271

The focus on truth telling was partially responsible for the original appeal of the psychological sciences among those in religion. Freud appeared as the psychological inheritor of Copernicus and Darwin, telling people the truths, not of earth's revolution around the sun or humanity's evolution from animal, but of the unconscious motivation of their overt behavior, social norms, and rationalizations. More recently, the regard for truth telling among those in pastoral theology is partially responsible for the attraction to liberation theories and theologies. Boisen and others asked the question of the meaning of religious struggles from within the midst of these struggles, focusing around the clinic and even Boisen's own flight into schizophrenia. In so doing, Boisen gave fresh visibility to the voice of the institutionalized patient. Liberation theologies ask a similar question, but further refined by demands for justice of a dramatic political nature (gender, ethnic, racial, class, and so forth). As Audre Lorde puts it: 'In my social location, where is justice struggling to be born and how can I help?'[38]

In the midst of the rich diversity of voices in theologies of liberation in *Lift Every Voice*, Engel and Thistlethwaite note a prominent commonalty in the first paragraph of their introduction: 'What these different theologies do share is their commitment to social justice', in essence their 'solidarity with those suffering and in need' in particular contexts. This entails the attempt to speak 'with and on behalf' rather than 'to or for' certain communities. It entails a 'crucial shift in the role of theologian from individual scholarly authority to reflective community advocate'. This shift is evident in the collaborative work that hopes to evolve a more 'communally-based and authorized theology', despite the general academic disdain for collectively-authored publications.[39]

---

[38] Audre Lorde, 'The Master's Tools Will Never Dismantle the Master's House,' in Cherrie Moraga and Gloria Anzaldúa (eds.), *This Bridge Called My Back: Writings by Radical Women of Color* (Watertown, MA, Persephone, 1981), p. 100, cited by Mary Potter Engel and Susan Thistlethwaite, *Lift Every Voice: Constructing Theologies from the Underside* (New York, Harper & Row, 1990), p. 14.

[39] Thistlethwaite and Engel, 'Introduction,' in *Lift Every Voice*, pp. 1-2.

Advocacy is not new to religious and theological studies: Bonhoeffer defines the study of religion as a two-fold exploration of the knowledge and experience that human evil will have its day alongside the insistence that it is the responsibility of each human being, especially if Christian or in some other way religiously committed, to prevent evil from having its day. Perhaps the focus has sharpened slightly in current practical theological circles: the focus, as Smith identifies it, is struggle and survival in the midst of suffering rather than enlightenment and transformation in the midst of privilege and power.

Problems and Possibilities

The evolving definitions of the study of pastoral theology as a practical theological discipline portend problems and possibilities. I will only name a few questions that arise from the precarious position of pastoral theology as a discipline peculiarly poised between practice, person, psychology, liberation theology, confessional religious congregations, and the academy. Tracy identifies three publics for which those in religion write: academy, society, and church.[40] More than any other area in the study of religion, those in pastoral and practical theology often attempt to speak and write for all three. Is this impossible or simply wrong-headed? Or does this bring critical relevance to the exercise?

This cross-public audience is not a new phenomenon; perhaps historically those in religion who have worked in ways analogous to the field of pastoral theology today also addressed multiple publics. However, a chief difference today is the striking divisions between these three publics in terms of language, standards of truth, practices and rituals, and norms. To write for all three publics has become more difficult than before. The tensions are heightened by United States universities whose standards empha-

---

[40] David Tracy, *The Analogical Imagination: Christian Theology and the Culture of Pluralism* (New York, Crossroad, 1981), p. 5.

size 'efficiency' and 'effectiveness' measured by quantitative standards. Not surprisingly, problems of identity, definitions, and clarity about the parameters plague the field. Moreover, within the academy of religion itself, a field that necessarily draws on a variety of other areas of study, from early Jewish and Christian studies to recent history of religion in America, ethics, and systematic theology, tends to do many tasks poorly rather than one task well. What are the foundational texts internal to the field, if significant resources are either suffering moments, science, or other religious texts? And who reads our texts? If only those in the church public buy and read them, how will scholars further theoretical reflection? Finally, the field joins other fields in arbitrating the tension between the particularity of religious and philosophical traditions and the claims to universality of theological and ethical discourse. If particularity determines truth, what of wider, possibly universal religious and moral claims?[41]

At the same time, could the field's struggles with marginalization and confusion also be the field's gift to the study of religion? From a disadvantageous position on the brink of academic discourse, the field offers a few strengths to current religious and theological studies. The field of pastoral theology has a long, complicated history adjudicating questions of interdisciplinary work – the use of the human sciences – within the study of religion. Such interdisciplinary study has begun to characterize almost all areas. Second, the field has an important history of attention to thick description of religious phenomenon, praxis, experience, including attention to the complexities of marginalized experience. Finally, over against ideals, which climaxed in the mid-twentieth-century, that religion could be, and perhaps should be, studied by non-participants, the field cannot avoid difficult questions about the place of faith and religious conviction in the study of religion as an element of the context in which the scholar-teacher herself is often located.

---

[41] See Lisa Sowle Cahill and James F. Childress, *Christian Ethics: Problems and Prospects* (Cleveland, Pilgrim, 1996).

These three general contributions by no means prove that pastoral theology has answers to current research questions on these matters. Rather, simply stated, pastoral theology is 'looking at both sides', 'always turning the surface over ... not being afraid to belly through darkness or cut through any weedy tangle of thread-roots'. Pastoral theologians have the dubious honor, as Larry Graham remarks, of being 'among the first to show up and among the last to "give answers"'.[42]

---

[42] Larry Kent Graham, *Familiar Strangers: Disclosing the Image of God Through Narratives of Care with Lesbian and Gay Men* (Philadelphia, Westminster/John Knox, forthcoming 1997), Introduction, 'Pastoral Theology and Gay and Lesbian Experience' (ms. p. 1). On the one hand, pastoral theologians attempt to 'be present to' the suffering, while on the other they press what is heard into 'constructive religious interpretation.' He reflects Hiltner's own position that 'unaddressed theological issues often arise from the particularity of human experience' and, if pressed, interpretation of what happens in concrete experience has the potential for constructing new theological understandings or clarifying unresolved matters in the tradition (cites Seward Hiltner, *Preface to Pastoral Theology* (Nashville, Abingdon, 1958).

List of contributors

Denise M. Ackermann holds the chair in Practical Theology at the University of the Western Cape, South Africa, where she also teaches courses in feminist theologies. She has published numerous articles and edited a book, together with J. Draper and E. Mashinini, entitled *Women Hold up Half the Sky: Women in the Church in Southern Africa* (Cluster Publications 1991), a first of its kind. She is currently working on a book which will appear in 1998 and which deals with the theological implications of the current post-apartheid process of truth-telling and reconciliation from a feminist perspective.

Riet Bons-Storm teaches practical theology and has a chair in Womenstudies and Pastoral Theology at the University of Groningen, the Netherlands. She has published several books in Dutch on pastoral theology and care from a feminist perspective, as well as numerous articles on the subject in Dutch, English and German. Her most recent book is: *The Incredible Woman. Listening to Women's Silences in Pastoral Care and Counseling*, (Abingdon Press, 1996).

Pamela D.Couture is the Director of the Faculty Research Center at the Association of Theological Schools in the United States and Canada, located in Pittsburgh, Pennsylvania. She previously taught pastoral care at Candler School of Theology, Emory University. She is author of *Blessed are the Poor? Women's Poverty, Family Policy, and Practical Theology* (Abingdon, 1991); co-editor of *Pastoral Care and Social Conflict* (Abingdon, 1995); and co-author of *From Conflict to Common Ground: Religion and the American Family Debate* (Westminster/John Knox Press, 1997).

Nancy Eiesland is assistant professor of Sociology of Religion at Candler School of Theology at Emory University, Atlanta GA, USA. Her work in practical theology includes *The Disabled God: Toward a Liberatory Theology of Disability* (Abingdon, 1994), and a forthcoming work of which she is co-author, entitled: *Human Disability and the Service of God: Theological Perspectives on Disability*

(Abingdon). She is author of numerous sociological works, including articles on women converts to classical pentacostalism and a forthcoming book on religion and urban change, entitled: *A Particular Place: Exurbanization and Religious Response in a Southern Town*.

Elaine L.Graham is lecturer in Social and Pastoral Theology at the University of Manchester, England, and Director of the Centre for Religion, Culture and Gender. Her chief academic interests lie at the interface of social theory and theology, particularly theories of gender and their implications for Christian faith practice. She has written several books on this subject.

Carol Lakey Hess, currently assistant professor of Christian Education at Princeton Theological Seminary, USA, is the author of *Caretakers of our Common House: Women's Development in Communities of Faith* (Abingdon, 1997). Her articles include: 'Education as an Art of Getting Dirty with Dignity', in Christie Neuger, (ed.), *The Arts of Ministry: Feminist and Womanist Approaches*. She is currently working on an understanding of community life based on a Reformed feminist theology of the Spirit of God. She is also involved in youth and adult education in the church and remains active in the prison ministry described in the essay.

Bonnie J. Miller-McLemore is associate professor of Pastoral Theology at Vanderbilt University Divinity School, Nashville, Tn. USA. She has published several articles and the books: *Death, Sin and the Moral Life: Contemporary Cultural Interpretations of Death* (Scholars Press, 1988) and *Also A Mother: Work and Family as Theological Dilemma* (Abingdon, 1994).

Barbara Nicholas is a feminist theologian from New Zealand. She has a number of occupations. Trained in microbiology and later theology, she has taught high school maths and science, and been involved in the Women's Refuge movement, in preschool education and in various church initiatives for social justice. All these strands of her life came together in doctorate studies in Bioethics, and she now teaches Bioethics at Otago medical school.